OXFORD
UNIVERSITY PRESS

Blackstone's Police Sergeants' and Inspectors' Mock Examination Paper 2010

Pack 1

OXFORD
UNIVERSITY PRESS

Great Clarendon Street, Oxford OX2 6DP

Oxford University Press is a department of the University of Oxford.
It furthers the University's objective of excellence in research, scholarship,
and education by publishing worldwide in

Oxford New York

Auckland Cape Town Dar es Salaam Hong Kong Karachi
Kuala Lumpur Madrid Melbourne Mexico City Nairobi
New Delhi Shanghai Taipei Toronto

With offices in

Argentina Austria Brazil Chile Czech Republic France Greece
Guatemala Hungary Italy Japan Poland Portugal Singapore
South Korea Switzerland Thailand Turkey Ukraine Vietnam

Oxford is a registered trade mark of Oxford University Press
in the UK and in certain other countries

Published in the United States
by Oxford University Press Inc., New York

First published 2004
Sixth edition published 2009

British Library Cataloguing in Publication Data

Data available

Typeset by Macmillan Publishing Solutions
Printed in Great Britain
on acid-free paper by
Ashford Colour Press Limited, Gosport, Hampshire

ISBN 978-0-19-957839-9

1 3 5 7 9 10 8 6 4 2

Acknowledgements

I would like to thank Peter Daniell, Katie Heath and Jodi Towler (at Oxford University Press) for their continued and highly professional support and assistance in the production of this product.

Above all, I thank my wife, Kate, for giving me the utmost encouragement and self-belief without which none of this would ever have happened.

Paul Connor

Introduction to the Mock Examination

Every single question in this mock examination is based on the syllabuses for the Part I sergeants' and inspectors' examinations of 2010.

Whilst this mock exam offers a useful means to test your knowledge and understanding of the OSPRE Part I syllabus, the content itself should not be considered indicative of the 'live' examination. Each question has been created from relevant material contained in the four-volume Blackstone's Police Manuals for 2010 (Crime, Evidence and Procedure, Road Policing and General Police Duties). These Manuals are the basis for both of the Part I examinations that will take place in 2010. As a result, **whatever Part I examination you are taking**, you can be sure that each question in this mock examination is a valid test of your knowledge and understanding of the law as all of the questions will directly relate to the material that you have studied for the examination.

*'How can this mock examination be suitable for **both** sets of candidates?'*

It is important to highlight that the lion's share of the material studied by sergeants' and inspectors' candidates is **exactly the same**. The main difference between the syllabuses is that the inspectors' syllabus is slightly smaller. However, while certain areas of the Road Policing Manual are excluded from the inspectors' syllabus, the material that sergeants' and inspectors' candidates have to study from the Crime, Evidence and Procedure and General Police Duties Manuals is **no different**.

In order to make this examination relevant to both sets of candidates, there will be no questions asked on those areas from Road Policing that are excluded from the inspectors' syllabus. At this point, sergeants' candidates may think that the examination is less relevant to them; but this is not so. I have simply excluded certain parts of the syllabus in favour of more commonly questioned areas from both syllabuses. Therefore, there are no questions in the mock examination based on the following chapters:

Chapter 3.1—Classification and Concepts
Chapter 3.3—Notices of Intended Prosecution
Chapter 3.10—Driver Licensing
Chapter 3.11—Fixed Penalty System
Chapter 3.12—Forgery and Falsification of Documents

My analysis of the last six sergeants' examinations shows that these excluded chapters collectively represent an average of seven questions per examination. Not being questioned on these areas does not make this examination any less valuable to the sergeants' candidate. As you will discover, the scope of the examination is still huge and I have still managed to cover a great many subjects within the 150 multiple-choice questions.

In order to test your knowledge in a realistic simulation of the Part I examination you will sit in 2010, I have allocated the multiple-choice questions on the basis below:

Volume 1	**Crime**	41 Questions
Volume 2	**Evidence and Procedure**	42 Questions
Volume 3	**Road Policing**	23 Questions
Volume 4	**General Police Duties**	44 Questions

I do not suggest the examination that you will take during 2010 will be a mirror image of this. However, in the last six sergeants' examinations and the last five inspectors' examinations there has been a noticeable trend towards testing less on Road Policing matters and more on Crime, Evidence and Procedure and General Police Duties. To make this examination a more practical revision tool, I have written an examination that reflects your examiners' **general** approach to question allocation.

As the range of the four Manuals is significant, I have set questions across a broad spectrum of the syllabuses; this makes the examination as fair a test of your overall ability as is possible. Some areas have been allocated several questions, e.g. everybody's 'banker' subjects, *'Drink, Drugs and Driving'* and *'Custody Officer's Duties'*. This means that the mock examination is a reasonable reflection of the content of the Manuals.

A by-product of this approach is that some of the questions in the mock examination may appear to relate to obscure or rarely used pieces of legislation. Historically, this is the source of many candidate complaints about the examination proper and the reason for the often heard criticism; *'It's not based on reality'* has been levelled year after year at the Part I examination process. What candidates need to remember is that the examination is not about the 'reality' of day-to-day policing; it is a test of an individual's knowledge and understanding of the law contained in the syllabuses. These questions should not be treated with contempt just because a candidate has never dealt with a particular offence or feels that it is unimportant; any such approach would be unwise. Remember that the Part I examinations are based on the sergeants' and inspectors' syllabuses and therefore everything contained within those syllabuses is potentially testable. The page telling candidates about the offence of burglary weighs exactly the same as the page telling candidates about Protocol 1, Article 3 of the European Convention on Human Rights and a correct mark for a question based on either subject is, like the weight of the page, worth exactly the same.

The distribution of the questions on the four Manuals is structured so that at no stage of the mock examination will you find yourself answering ten questions in a row on Road Policing or Crime, etc.

Most importantly, the style of the questions in the mock examination matches the style of question that you will face in the examination proper. You cannot accurately assess your knowledge, understanding and application of the law if you are not testing it in the same way as you will be tested in your examination. Many of you will have seen questions that offer complex choices as answers to multiple-choice questions, for example:

PARKER breaks into a warehouse intending to steal anything of value that he can find. He forces a door and gets into the warehouse but finds nothing during his search. Frustrated at his lack of success, PARKER damages a toilet inside the warehouse before he leaves.

What offences does PARKER commit?

(i)   Burglary contrary to s. 9(1)(a) of the Theft Act 1968.
(ii)   Burglary contrary to s. 9(1)(b) of the Theft Act 1968.
(iii)   Attempted theft contrary to s. 1 of the Criminal Attempts Act 1981.
(iv)   Criminal damage contrary to s. 1(1) of the Criminal Damage Act 1971.

A (i), (ii) and (iv) only.
B (ii) and (iii) only.
C (i) and (iv) only.
D (ii), (iii) and (iv) only.

or:

In which, if either, of the following cases has an offence of obstruct police, contrary to s. 89 of the Police Act 1996, been committed?

(i) STEVENS is caught in a speed trap. After he is given a speeding ticket he doubles back and drives 200 metres away from the speed trap. He holds out a homemade sign that states, 'All drivers slow down—Police speed trap ahead!'

(ii) INGLETON is stopped by PC CONNOLLY who believes INGLETON may have seen the direction in which an armed robber has run off. INGLETON refuses to answer any of the questions put to him by the officer.

A (i) only.
B (ii) only.
C Both.
D Neither.

The format of these questions **IS NOT** what you will face in your examination in 2010. These are acceptable question styles but they are not approved by the Police Promotions Examination Board for use in Part I examinations. The style you will face in your Part I examination is as below:

BREEN plans an armed robbery on a security van that regularly picks up cash at a local bank. He enlists the help of FISH and TODD who agree to actually carry out the armed robbery while BREEN waits for them at a rendezvous point. BREEN has no intention of taking part in the commission of the armed robbery itself. Unknown to BREEN, the security company has been 'tipped off' about the robbery and changes the day of collection so that the security van does not arrive at the bank. FISH and TODD leave empty-handed.

Does BREEN commit statutory conspiracy contrary to s. 1 of the Criminal Law Act 1977?

A No, BREEN has no intention of taking part in the actual armed robbery itself.
B Yes, BREEN commits the offence as soon as he plans the robbery and before he enlists the help of FISH and TODD.

C No, the commission of the offence is impossible because the security van would never arrive at the bank.

D Yes, BREEN has agreed on a course of conduct that will involve the commission of an offence.

Now that you are familiar with how and why the mock examination has been produced and written, it is appropriate to consider the benefits of taking the examination: this is primarily to be able to assess your performance accurately. This can, in turn, help you in a number of ways:

1. It may highlight areas of weakness (for example, your knowledge of Road Policing may not be as good as you think it is).

2. It may highlight areas of strength (for example, your knowledge of Crime may be stronger than you think it is).

A direct consequence of the above two points is that the mock examination could help you channel your revision into more productive areas of your syllabus.

3. It is a good test of your ability to deal with 150 questions in a three-hour period. The pressure of dealing with a question once every 72 seconds (the average time per question) can be intense. Will you be able to cope with it? Will you have to take steps to increase the pace of your question answering in order to complete the exam proper? On the other hand, did you finish with a great deal of time to spare? If so, are you giving the questions enough thought before answering?

I cannot stress enough how important this benefit is. A colleague of mine provides an all-too-familiar unfortunate but real-life case study. He sat the sergeants' examination but ran out of time with 20 questions left to answer; he did not even have time to guess the answers and consequently lost all of those marks. Unsurprisingly he failed the examination. Even if he had had time to hurriedly fill in the last 20 boxes this is a far from ideal situation. Those 20 questions were worth a possible 14% of his final mark and were too much to sacrifice when targeting the 55% or 65% pass mark. I know it may be difficult to follow my instructions, i.e. to allocate three hours and stick to it, but I believe that this practice is invaluable. What a waste of your revision effort to fail, not because of a lack of knowledge, but because your timekeeping was at fault.

4. Answering multiple-choice questions is one of the best methods of testing your knowledge.

5. The preparation involved in practising a full examination will assist in building your confidence to deal with the examination proper.

6. It will improve your exam technique by allowing you to see how easy it is to make a mistake, either by failing to read the question correctly or by reading too much into the question.

However you perform in the mock examination, I would strongly advise that you do not read too much into your result. Failing or passing this examination does not warrant despair or joy; this mock examination is primarily intended to give you practice and is not a predictor of performance in the examination proper.

I hope that your efforts are rewarded and wish you every success in your 2010 Part I examination.

Paul Connor

Instructions for Completion

READ THE WHOLE OF THE INSTRUCTIONS BEFORE ATTEMPTING THE MOCK EXAMINATION

If you want to get the most from this mock examination then you must treat it as if you were sitting the examination proper.

Time

You have up to three hours to complete the examination. It might not take you that long but it is best to assume that it will, so please make absolutely sure that you set aside three hours. You cannot expect to sit part of the examination for one hour, take a break for 20 minutes, return to the examination and then get an accurate picture of your performance. The examination must be completed in one three-hour sitting. If you want to, why not try and complete the examination between 10.00 am and 1.00 pm, as this is the time period you will sit the examination proper in 2010.

Environment

You need to be able to concentrate on the examination and you cannot do that if the television is on, the phone is ringing, etc. Find a place where you will not be disturbed for the three hours this examination will take and make sure that there are no distractions that will affect your performance.

Equipment

Ideally you will sit at a single desk to take the examination, but I appreciate that in most cases this will not be possible. However, you will need a table and chair of some description. Trying to fill out the answer sheet on your lap whilst holding the question paper open will prove to be a difficult task to say the least.

Make sure that you can see a clock, stopwatch or wristwatch. It would be best to have two timepieces, just in case one stops.

You will need two pencils, a pencil sharpener and an eraser.

Pack 1

In Pack 1 you will find a blank answer sheet and the question booklet. Place both documents on the table.

When you decide to start the examination, please open the question booklet. Work through the test questions and make your choice of A, B, C or D by putting a horizontal line through the corresponding letter on the answer sheet.

Do not make any notes or doodles on the answer sheet. If you wish to make any marks, do so on the question booklet.

Only mark one answer for each question. If two or more choices are made then the question would be marked as incorrect in the examination proper.

Make sure that if you change your answer you erase the previous mark fully.

If you leave an answer blank then it would be marked incorrect in the examination proper. Try not to leave blank answers when you are unsure. Mark an answer and come back to the question if you have time at the end of the examination.

Pack 2

When you have finished the examination, open Pack 2 and begin the marking process. When you have finished marking your paper, please refer to the answer booklet for a detailed explanation of the correct answers with paragraph references to the *Blackstone's Police Manuals 2010*.

The marking process will take some time—to ensure accuracy, please do not rush this stage!

OXFORD
UNIVERSITY PRESS

Blackstone's Police Sergeants' and Inspectors' Mock Examination Paper 2010

Question Booklet

Time Allowed—180 minutes

1. Each of the questions is followed by four possible answers, only ONE of which is correct. Choose the ONE response that you consider to be correct. On the answer sheet mark the box that corresponds to your selection. Mark your answer clearly with a — mark. The answer sheet has spaces for your answers to all questions. If you change your mind about an answer, rub out the first mark, then mark your new answer. Mark only one answer for each question.

2. You are reminded that there is no need to read the whole examination paper before beginning to select answers to the questions posed.

3. You must ensure that BEFORE the close of the examination, all of your answers to the questions have been correctly entered on the answer sheet. If you leave a question unanswered for any reason, it will not receive a mark.

4. You may make any notes you wish on the question papers.

1. ROTHEN is driving his Vauxhall Astra along a road when PC SIMPSON (who is on uniform foot patrol) steps out into the road and causes ROTHEN to stop his car. When ROTHEN stops his car, the front offside wheel accidentally stops on PC SIMPSON's foot, crushing the officer's foot in the process and causing extensive bruising. PC SIMPSON screams in pain and shouts at ROTHEN to move his car. ROTHEN realises PC SIMPSON has been hurt and, reckless as to whether keeping the car on the officer's foot will cause injury, replies 'No, you asked me to stop so you can wait for a minute!'

   Considering the law in relation to ROTHEN's criminal conduct and the law of assaults, which of the statements below is correct?

   A ROTHEN will commit an offence of s. 47 assault (Offences Against the Person Act 1861) against PC SIMPSON but only after he refuses to move his car from the officer's foot.
   B ROTHEN has not committed an offence in respect of assaults as he did not have the requisite *mens rea* for any assault when he initially drove onto the officer's foot and caused injury.
   C The moment ROTHEN causes the injury to PC SIMPSON by driving onto the officer's foot he will commit an offence of common assault/battery (contrary to s. 39 of the Criminal Justice Act 1988).
   D As ROTHEN was only reckless as to whether keeping the car on PC SIMPSON's foot would cause injury, he commits no offence in respect of assault.

2. DCs McKINNON and GLAZE execute a search warrant (under s. 8 of the Police and Criminal Evidence Act 1984) at the home address of ACLAND in respect of allegations that ACLAND is involved in the making and distribution of child pornography. It quickly becomes apparent that there is a large amount of material in ACLAND's loft that relates to these allegations including several dozen large crates packed full of ordinary magazines that have child pornography material mixed into them. ACLAND also has a computer in the loft which is turned on and has a pornographic picture of a small child on the screen. The officers believe that there is further pornographic material stored on the computer.

   With regard to the officers' powers under s. 50 of the Criminal Justice and Police Act 2001 (seize and sift powers), which of the following comments is true?

   A The officers can only exercise these powers if an officer of the rank of inspector or above authorises them to do so.
   B The powers would allow the officers to seize the crates containing magazines and pictures and the computer if it were essential to do so.
   C In this situation the officers did not require a s. 8 PACE warrant to search ACLAND's address as they could have searched it under the powers provided by s. 50 of the Criminal Justice and Police Act 2001.
   D In order to use the powers, the officers will have to show that it was convenient and preferable to do so considering the nature and quality of the material recovered in the search.

3. AMES is a security guard who has just picked up a bag of cash from a supermarket. There is approximately £2,500 cash in the bag and this is the property of the supermarket. AMES is walking towards his transit van when he is approached by JOFEMAR and STAFFORD who intend to steal the cash. JOFEMAR nudges into AMES using a slight amount of force to knock him off-balance, and as contact is made AMES drops the bag of cash to the pavement. STAFFORD picks up the bag of cash and he and JOFEMAR run from the scene. Several minutes later the police arrive and a description of the two men is quickly circulated by radio. PC BLAKE is on patrol several streets away from the scene of the offence and sees JOFEMAR and STAFFORD walking towards him. PC BLAKE approaches the men and, as he does so, JOFEMAR produces a knife and tells the officer to stay back or be stabbed; both men escape.

    With regard to the offence of robbery (contrary to s. 8 of the Theft Act 1968), which of the following comments is true?

    A   A robbery has not taken place as the force used was not against the victim of the theft.
    B   This would not constitute an offence of robbery as the amount of force used to knock AMES off-balance was only slight.
    C   The offence of robbery is first committed when STAFFORD picks up the bag of cash.
    D   The offence of robbery is first committed when JOFEMAR produces a knife and tells PC BLAKE to stand back or be stabbed.

4. Section 7 of the Road Traffic Act 1988 deals with the provision of specimens for analysis for drink/drive related offences.

    Which of the following comments is correct with regard to that section?

    A   A requirement to provide a specimen of breath can only be made at a police station.
    B   Where a requirement for blood/urine is made under s. 7(3)(b) that sample must be used and the prosecution cannot revert to evidence produced by a breath sample.
    C   The fact that a person is too drunk to provide a breath specimen will not be regarded as a 'medical' reason for requiring a sample of blood/urine.
    D   In order to have reasonable cause to believe that medical reasons exist for taking a specimen of blood/urine instead of breath, a police officer must seek the advice of a doctor.

5. PC GOWEN arrested HOOPER for an offence of affray (contrary to s. 3 of the Public Order Act 1986). PC GOWEN decided to grant HOOPER 'street bail' under s. 30 of the Police and Criminal Evidence Act 1984 as amended by the Criminal Justice Act 2003. PC GOWEN provides HOOPER with a notice in writing stating that he is to attend Fronsby police station at 11.00hrs five days later. PC GOWEN also imposed a number of bail conditions on HOOPER including a condition that HOOPER's movements are restricted by a curfew between 20.00hrs and 06.00hrs. The day after HOOPER was given bail, he is successful in a job interview at a bakery; the job requires him to begin work at 04.00hrs. HOOPER wishes to have his bail conditions altered so that he can carry out his new job.

Which one of the statements below is correct?

A HOOPER must attend at Fronsby police station and speak to a relevant officer to vary the conditions of bail.
B HOOPER's bail conditions can only be varied by the officer who originally granted him bail, i.e. PC GOWEN.
C HOOPER can attend at any police station in the force area where he was arrested and bailed to have the conditions altered.
D HOOPER can only have his bail conditions varied by a magistrates' court.

6. PC BAINES is on uniform patrol when he is approached by DONEGAN who tells the officer that he has just seen MATTHEWS driving a car at speed along a nearby road. DONEGAN states that he heard a loud bang as MATTHEWS drove along the road and thinks that MATTHEWS has struck a parked car. PC BAINES believes that an accident has taken place and several minutes later PC BAINES stops the car driven by MATTHEWS.

In relation to procedures following an accident (under s. 6(5) of the Road Traffic Act 1988), can PC BAINES require MATTHEWS to take a preliminary breath test?

A No, because an accident must have actually taken place. PC BAINES' belief that an accident has taken place is not enough to make the requirement.
B Yes, but the preliminary breath test can only take place at or near the place where the requirement to co-operate with the test is imposed.
C No, as PC BAINES must believe or suspect that MATTHEWS has been drinking.
D Yes, but only if PC BAINES reasonably believes that MATTHEWS has failed to stop at the scene of an accident.

7. WALTON has been arrested in connection with an offence of possessing indecent images of children (contrary to s. 1 of the Protection of Children Act 1978) and a s. 18 PACE search of WALTON's home address has been authorised. PC EAGAN is one of several officers who take part in the search. While PC EAGAN is searching WALTON's study, he finds several pictures of animated cartoon characters. One picture illustrates a cartoon male character having anal sex with a cartoon female corpse. PC EAGAN also finds real-life pictures of WALTON where WALTON is taking part in sexual intercourse with a sheep.

Considering the offence of possession of extreme pornographic images (contrary to s. 63 of the Criminal Justice and Immigration Act 2008), which of the statements below is correct?

A WALTON only commits the offence in respect of the picture of the cartoon male character having sex with the cartoon female corpse.

B WALTON only commits the offence in respect of the real-life photographs of him having sexual intercourse with the sheep.

C WALTON commits the offence in respect of both the cartoon image and the real-life images.

D The offence is not committed as cartoon characters are not covered by the legislation and the real-life pictures show WALTON and not another person, directly participating in the bestiality.

8. PS BRENNAN is the supervisor of a group of constables who have recently received instruction regarding the contents of the Race Relations Act 1976. The constables are discussing the Act and its implications and PS BRENNAN joins in with the conversation. During the discussion several comments are made regarding the Act and surrounding case law which PS BRENNAN will need to correct.

Which of the following comments is the only one to show a correct understanding of the Act?

A The Race Relations Act aims to control discrimination on several grounds, amongst which are sexuality and religion.

B Discrimination on the grounds of ethnic group is covered and this includes Rastafarians.

C Speakers of a particular language (e.g. Welsh) are an ethnic group *per se*.

D The Race Relations Act 1976 aims to control discrimination on the grounds of national origins.

9. DANCE has been arrested for an offence of theft and during her subsequent interview she denied the offence. After consultation it is decided that DANCE will be charged with the offence. Before DANCE is charged it is proposed to obtain a photograph of her.

With regard to the Police and Criminal Evidence Act and Code 'D' of the Codes of Practice, which of the following statements is correct?

A As DANCE has not been charged with the offence, she cannot be photographed unless an officer of the rank of inspector or above authorises the taking of a photograph.

B DANCE can be photographed but that photograph must be taken by a constable.

C DANCE can be photographed but it must be by a constable or designated detention officer of the same sex as DANCE.

D DANCE can be photographed and if necessary the photograph can be taken using reasonable force.

10. PUGH is the licensee of the 'Wild Stag' public house and possesses a premises licence to sell alcohol to members of the public. PC NIXON is on foot patrol and walks past the 'Wild Stag' 10 minutes before the pub is due to open for lunchtime business. PC PUGH decides to enter the pub to see whether or not the licensed activities will be carried out in accordance with the authorisation.

Which of the statements below is correct?

A PC NIXON cannot enter the premises at this time, as they are not actually being used for licensable activities.
B The premises may only be entered if PC NIXON is investigating offences in relation to the premises.
C PC NIXON can enter the premises if they are about to be used for licensable activities.
D PC NIXON can enter the premises but only if he is accompanied by an 'authorised person'.

11. The Police and Criminal Evidence Act 1984 requires that prisoners who will be detained (or who are likely to be detained) for more than a certain period of time must go to a 'designated' police station.

What is that period of time?

A More than three hours.
B More than six hours.
C More than nine hours.
D More than twelve hours.

12. Section 1 of the Emergency Workers (Obstruction) Act 2006 covers behaviour whereby the obstruction of certain emergency workers without a reasonable excuse will constitute an offence.

Which of the individuals below would be protected by the legislation?

A A council worker responding to an emergency bridge repair.
B A member of Her Majesty's Coastguard responding to an emergency circumstance.
C A nurse in a hospital responding to an emergency in the Accident and Emergency ward.
D An employee of a private firm called out to repair a major electrical fault.

13. RAINWAY is a cleaner at a hotel and while cleaning a room being rented by TYLER, she finds a packet containing what she suspects to be an amount of cocaine. RAINWAY takes possession of the packet with the intention of preventing TYLER from committing an offence in connection with it and to deliver it into the custody of her local beat officer when she meets her in three days' time. Two days later, RAINWAY is searched by PC LEDGE in relation to an unconnected matter. During the course of the search, PC LEDGE finds the packet of cocaine.

Why will RAINWAY be unable to utilise the defence under s. 5(4) of the Misuse of Drugs Act 1971 to the offence of possession of a controlled drug (contrary to s. 5 of the Misuse of Drugs Act 1971)?

   A Because she did not take the drug with the intention of taking it to someone lawfully entitled to possess it as soon as possible after taking possession of it.
   B Because the defence is not available to a charge of possession of a controlled drug.
   C Because she did not have possession of the drug with the intention of destroying it.
   D Because the defence is not available to a charge of possession of a Class A drug.

14. ELEY has been arrested for an offence of burglary and is brought into a custody block where his details are taken by PS HOPKINS. It becomes apparent that ELEY is deaf but he can lip-read and his communication abilities are unaffected by his disability. ELEY tells PS HOPKINS that he is happy to be interviewed regarding the offence but he does not want an interpreter present in the inter-view room.

Which of the statements below is correct in respect of ELEY?

   A If there is any doubt about a person's hearing or speaking ability or they appear deaf, they must not be interviewed in the absence of an interpreter.
   B ELEY can be interviewed without an interpreter but he must agree on tape (audio or video) to being interviewed without one.
   C ELEY must not be interviewed in the absence of an interpreter unless he agrees in writing to being interviewed without one.
   D ELEY can be interviewed without an interpreter as long as an officer of the rank of inspector or above authorises it.

15. The test for racial or religious aggravation (for racially or religiously aggravated offences) is set out in s. 28 of the Crime and Disorder Act 1998. In addition to this test, only certain types of offences can be subject to the legislation.

With regard to the above factors, which of the following could be classed as a racially or religiously aggravated offence?

A PARKER commits an offence of causing grievous bodily harm with intent (contrary to s. 18 of the Offences Against the Person Act 1861) against SAWAR. The offence was motivated by hostility to the fact that SAWAR was a Muslim.

B BATEHAM commits an offence of causing actual bodily harm (contrary to s. 47 of the Offences Against the Person Act 1861) against CRAY. Immediately before the offence, BATEHAM demonstrates hostility towards CRAY based on the fact that CRAY is a Catholic.

C FABURUSO commits an offence of aggravated criminal damage (contrary to s. 1(2) of the Criminal Damage Act 1971) against the property and life of HANSON. The offence was motivated by hostility to the fact that HANSON is an atheist.

D NEALE commits an offence of affray (contrary to s. 3 of the Public Order Act 1986) against RUBIN. Immediately after the offence, NEALE demonstrates hostility towards RUBIN based on the fact that RUBIN is a Rastafarian.

16. Code D provides the definition of an 'intimate' and 'non-intimate' sample and also provides guidance on who may take an 'intimate' sample.

In which of the following circumstances has an intimate sample been taken by the correct person in order to comply with the Codes of Practice?

A A dental impression is taken from TASKER by HENSHAW, who is a registered medical practitioner.

B A swab is taken from a part of YATE's genitals by PS EALY.

C A sample is taken from under TRICKET's nail by ULLON, who is a registered nurse.

D A sample of urine is taken from LOPINE by PC FALLOW.

17. PC HANIA and PC GRAHAM are both interested in the role of the 'police friend' in misconduct or performance proceedings and are discussing the matter together. The officers make a number of comments about the 'police friend' only one of which is correct.

Considering the role of the 'police friend' which of those comments is correct?

A The police friend could be a member of police staff.

B The police friend cannot represent a police officer at a police appeals tribunal.

C If a police officer is interviewed in connection with a criminal matter committed whilst off duty which has no connection with his/her role as a serving police officer, the police friend has every right to attend the criminal interview of that police officer.

D A police friend who has agreed to accompany a police officer would not be considered 'on duty' when attending interviews, meetings or hearings.

18. KHATUN has been charged with an offence of attempted rape and the issue of bail is now being considered. KHATUN has a previous conviction for manslaughter, for which he served 5 years' imprisonment, that is 12 years old but he has no other previous convictions.

Will the provisions of s. 25 of the Criminal Justice and Public Order Act 1994 be applicable in these circumstances?

A Yes, as KHATUN will not be granted bail unless there are exceptional circumstances which justify it.

B No, as KHATUN's previous conviction for manslaughter is over 10 years old.

C Yes, due to the nature of the charge and because of KHATUN's previous conviction, he cannot be granted bail.

D No, as s. 25 only relates to defendants charged with murder, attempted murder or manslaughter.

19. HERRICK is an ardent supporter of the British National Party (BNP) and has arranged a meeting in a private function room at a hotel to rally support and discuss the policies of the party. The meeting is attended by several of HERRICK's associates. When the meeting begins and HERRICK addresses the group, SENNOR (a member of the hotel staff) enters the function room and shouts threats towards HERRICK causing HERRICK to fear harm to his person. The police are called and PC MAIN attends the scene. When the officer arrives, SENNOR is still in the function room and although no longer shouting insults, he states that he will not leave the room and that as soon as PC MAIN leaves, he will begin shouting threats at HERRICK again as the BNP's policies are offensive to any right-minded individual.

In respect of the common law offence of breach of the peace, which of the following comments is correct?

A PC MAIN should advise HERRICK to stop addressing the group as his words are antagonising SENNOR.

B A breach of the peace cannot take place in such a situation as the activity is taking place on private premises.

C SENNOR can be arrested for a breach of the peace.

D A breach of the peace can only take place on private property if it can be shown that members of the public outside the property are affected.

20. BALL is 15 years old and lives with her mother who has a residency order in respect of BALL. BALL's father, HUDSON, wants to take BALL to Scotland for a two-week holiday but BALL's mother has unreasonably refused to allow HUDSON to take their daughter away on several occasions. Regardless of this refusal, HUDSON takes BALL to Scotland.

Has HUDSON committed an offence of child abduction (contrary to s. 1 of the Child Abduction Act 1984)?

A No, because BALL's mother has unreasonably refused to consent to the holiday.

B Yes, because there is a residency order in effect in respect of BALL.

C No, because HUDSON has not taken BALL out of the United Kingdom.

D Yes, because BALL's mother does not consent to the holiday.

21. During a custody officers' course, four newly promoted sergeants are receiving training in respect of the issue of bail. Bail given under the Bail Act 1976 and the ramifications of the Police and Criminal Evidence Act 1984 in respect of bail are being discussed. A number of comments are made by the sergeants' during this discussion.

Which of the comments is correct?

A If a defendant is remanded in custody in respect of certain charges that are not ultimately pursued, then the police can be sued for damages (for the wrongful exercise of lawful authority) on the basis that the police had wrongly opposed bail.

B When considering the granting of bail, the custody officer must have regard to certain considerations listed in the Bail Act 1976; one of these considerations is the probable penalty for the offence with which the defendant is charged.

C Bail cannot be granted to an individual if the offence with which they are charged was committed outside England or Wales.

D The Police and Criminal Evidence Act 1984 places a maximum statutory time limit on the granting of bail; this time limit is two years.

22. PC PORTER is on uniform foot patrol when he is directed to an area where a burglary has just taken place. A description of the possible offender is circulated and while searching the area, PC PORTER sees MALIK, who matches the description circulated, walking towards him. PC PORTER decides to exercise his powers under s. 1 of the Police and Criminal Evidence Act 1984 and to search MALIK. When PC PORTER approaches and speaks to MALIK it becomes obvious that MALIK is having difficulty understanding what the officer is saying to him.

With regard to the Police and Criminal Evidence Act 1984, which of the statements below is correct?

A As MALIK does not appear to understand what is being said to him, PC PORTER cannot search him.

B PC PORTER must give MALIK certain information which can be communicated before or during the course of the search.

C As MALIK does not appear to understand what is being said, PC PORTER must take reasonable steps to bring all relevant information to his attention before starting the search.

D As MALIK is having difficulty understanding what PC PORTER is saying, the officer need not attempt to explain anything to him and he may search MALIK without communicating the usual information required.

23. CRANE has been arrested and charged with a robbery offence. The police area he has been arrested and charged in is covered by s. 63(B) of the Police and Criminal Evidence Act 1984 (providing that a sample of urine or a non-intimate sample may be taken from a person aged 14 or over in police detention for the purpose of ascertaining whether the individual has a specified Class A drug in his/her body). PS SHAW, the custody officer, has detained CRANE after charging him as he believes it is necessary to enable a sample to be taken (under s. 63(B) PACE).

In such a situation, how long may PS SHAW authorise CRANE to be kept in police detention for?

A A period not exceeding two hours beginning when CRANE was charged with the robbery offence.

B A period not exceeding four hours beginning when CRANE was charged with the robbery offence.

C A period not exceeding six hours beginning when CRANE was charged with the robbery offence.

D A period not exceeding eight hours beginning when CRANE was charged with the robbery offence.

24. TYRONE has a long-standing disagreement with PERCY and goes round to PERCY's house intending to cause trouble. TYRONE takes his two Doberman Pinscher dogs, who he has restrained on leads, with him to help him. He gets to PERCY's house and stands outside the front lounge window, staring into the house. At this stage he is not saying or doing anything. PERCY comes into his front room and sees TYRONE and his dogs and at this point TYRONE starts to shout '*PERCY is a wanker*' repeatedly towards PERCY. PERCY comes outside his house and approaches TYRONE who shouts '*Savage the bastard, boys!*' and makes to release his two dogs by shaking the dogs' leads. PERCY is frightened by TYRONE's actions. TYRONE has a good hold of the dogs and has no intention of actually releasing them on PERCY.

Which of the following statements is correct with regard to the offence of affray (contrary to s. 3 of the Public Order Act 1986)?

A An affray is first committed when TYRONE shouts '*Savage the bastard, boys!*' and makes to release his two dogs.

B An affray is first committed when TYRONE stands outside PERCY's house and shouts '*PERCY is a wanker*' repeatedly.

C An affray is first committed when TYRONE stands outside PERCY's front lounge window staring into the house.

D The offence of affray is not committed.

25. JORDAN is out walking along a public footpath. He decides to take a shortcut over a field next to the footpath even though there is a sign separating the field and footpath that clearly indicates that it is private land. As JORDAN is walking through the private field, he decides to pick some wild blackberries to make some jam for his own use. When JORDAN returns home he makes several pots of jam but realises he has made too much and decides to sell the surplus at a car boot sale. JORDAN takes the pots of jam to the car boot sale where he sells them for 25p per jar.

At what point, if at all, does JORDAN commit the offence of theft?

A When he picks the berries from the private land.
B When he decides to sell the surplus pots of jam.
C When he actually sells the jam at the car boot sale.
D The offence of theft is not committed.

26. Inspector JOYCE is involved in a serious car accident and receives injuries, which means she will be off work for a considerable period of time. In order to deal with the absence of Inspector JOYCE several officers need to be temporarily promoted. It is decided that a sergeant should be temporarily promoted to the rank of inspector and a constable will be temporarily promoted to the rank of sergeant (taking the place of the sergeant temporarily promoted to the rank of inspector).

Considering reg. 6 of the Police (Promotion) Regulations 1996, which of the statements below is true?

A A constable can be temporarily promoted to the rank of sergeant regardless of whether he/she is qualified for promotion to the rank under reg. 3.
B A sergeant can be temporarily promoted to the rank of inspector but only because a vacancy exists for an officer of that rank.
C A sergeant can be temporarily promoted to the rank of inspector regardless of the fact that he/she is not qualified to that rank under reg. 3.
D A constable can be temporarily promoted to the rank of sergeant but only if he/she is qualified for the promotion under reg. 3.

27. YAU is a friend of RICHARDSON. RICHARDSON asks YAU for a favour (as RICHARDSON has lost his driving licence) to drive RICHARDSON's Rolls Royce Corniche as his chauffeur for a day. YAU agrees and meets RICHARDSON at RICHARDSON's business premises where he is assured by RICHARDSON that the vehicle has all the relevant legal documentation, including an insurance policy. This is not the case and the vehicle has no insurance. RICHARDSON tells YAU that the Rolls Royce is parked in a public car park opposite RICHARDSON's business premises and gives the keys to the vehicle to YAU. YAU goes to the car park and drives the vehicle from the third storey, through the car park and into the street. As he drives in the road between the car park and RICHARDSON's business premises, he is involved in a damage-only accident.

Considering the law with regard to the offence of using a motor vehicle without insurance (contrary to s. 143 of the Road Traffic Act 1988), which of the following statements is true?

A Although YAU has committed the offence, he will have a defence as he has been assured by RICHARDSON that the vehicle had insurance and he had no reason to believe that such a policy was not in force.

B YAU has committed the offence which is punishable by a fine and a minimum mandatory disqualification period of three months.

C YAU has committed the offence for which there is no defence.

D YAU commits the offence when driving the vehicle in the car park.

28. MUNRO has been charged with a burglary and pleads 'not guilty'. Primary and secondary disclosure has been made by the prosecution and the case goes to trial. One day before MUNRO's trial, a scenes of crime report relating to the burglary is found. The report states that a finger-mark was found at the crime scene but cannot be identified as belonging to MUNRO.

Considering the duties of the prosecutor in relation to disclosure, which of the statements below is correct?

A It is the opinion of the prosecutor that is relevant. If he/she expects that the finger-mark would not assist the defence then it need not be disclosed and the Criminal Procedure and Investigations Act 1996 has been complied with.

B A finger-mark that cannot be identified is classed as 'negative information' and need not be disclosed by the prosecution.

C The finger-mark should be disclosed as there is a continuing duty on the prosecutor to disclose any material reasonably considered capable of undermining the prosecution case or assisting the case of the accused.

D As the prosecution has made a secondary disclosure to the defence, the Criminal Procedure and Investigations Act 1996 has been complied with and there is no need to inform the defence about the finger-mark.

29. GRASTER breaks into a house intending to steal anything he can whilst inside. He smashes a window to the house and enters the lounge. While he is looking around for anything to steal he hears a noise from the upstairs of the house and thinking it could be the occupier he grabs hold of the first thing he can, a letter opener, and decides that anyone who stands in his way will be stabbed with it. Nothing more happens after the noise but GRASTER decides to hold on to the letter opener just in case. He finds £200.00 cash in the lounge and steals it. He moves from the lounge into a dining room but finds nothing more to steal and decides to leave the house.

At what stage, if at all, does GRASTER first commit an offence of aggravated burglary (contrary to s. 10 of the Theft Act 1968)?

A When he picks up the letter opener to use it to stab someone if anyone stands in his way.
B When he steals the £200.00 in cash.
C When he moves from the lounge into the dining room.
D The offence has not been committed in these circumstances.

30. SMITH believes that the activites of al-Qaeda are justified because of the British and American action in Iraq. He publishes an article on the Internet that glorifies the actions of terrorists such as the London bombers, stating that what they did was right and proper and that further similar attacks would be justified.

Considering the offence of publishing a statement to encourage the commission, preparation or instigation of acts of terrorism (contrary to s. 1(2) of the Terrorism Act 2006), which of the following statements is correct?

A This offence cannot be committed by publishing a statement electronically, i.e. via the Internet.
B SMITH could be served with a notice requiring the modification or removal of the statement.
C This offence is punishable with a maximum term of imprisonment of 10 years.
D This offence can only be committed in the United Kingdom and a prosecution requires the permission of the Attorney General.

31. KACHANSKI (who is 13 years old) is convicted of an offence of burglary. A parenting order is made in respect of KACHANSKI to give his parents more help and support to change their child's criminal behaviour.

What is the maximum period that KACHANSKI's parents could be ordered to comply with the parenting order for?

A A period not exceeding 12 months.
B A period not exceeding 18 months.
C A period not exceeding 24 months.
D A period not exceeding 36 months.

32. PS HARVARD is the immediate supervisor of PC SCOATES. PS HARVARD has received several minor complaints from members of the public about the attitude and rudeness of PC SCOATES when she was dealing with them; PS HARVARD has also noticed several issues with the officer's attitude and abrupt behaviour in the police station. PS HARVARD has mentioned this to PC SCOATES on a number of occasions and there seems to be no reason for the officer's continued rudeness and bad attitude. A further complaint is received from a member of the public about rude behaviour by the officer and PS HARVARD decides that a 'UPP' (Unsatisfactory Police Performance) meeting should be held with PC SCOATES under the Police (Performance) Regulations 2008.

Which of the statements below is correct regarding the first stage of such a UPP procedure?

A The first stage of a UPP procedure must be managed by an officer of at least the rank of inspector.

B PS HARVARD can ask a human resources professional to attend the UPP to advise him on the proceedings at the first stage meeting.

C If PS HARVARD issues an improvement notice to PC SCOATES, its 'specified period' would not normally exceed one month but, in exceptional circumstances, it can be extended to a maximum period of six months.

D PC SCOATES does not have a right of appeal in respect of any improvement notice imposed by PS HARVARD at a first stage meeting.

33. BURNELL is having an affair with COSGRIFF's wife. COSGRIFF discovers this and goes to BURNELL's house intending to assault him. When COSGRIFF arrives at BURNELL's house, BURNELL is getting into his car. COSGRIFF runs towards the car and on seeing COSGRIFF, BURNELL jumps into his car and locks all the doors. COSGRIFF knocks on the car door window and shouts, *'If you don't get out of that car I'm gonna smash the window and break your fuckin' neck!'* BURNELL hears the threat and fearing that he will be assaulted he calls the police. PC OWEN arrives and on her arrival COSGRIFF moves away from the car. BURNELL tells the officer what has happened, at which point COSGRIFF shouts, *'You're lucky the little cop's here or I'd kick the shit out of you!'*

With regard to the above circumstances and the two statements made by COSGRIFF, which of the remarks below is correct?

A The only time that COSGRIFF commits an offence of assault is when he threatens BURNELL in the presence of PC OWEN.

B COSGRIFF commits an assault when he threatens BURNELL in his car and when he threatens him in the presence of PC OWEN.

C COSGRIFF does not commit an offence of assault in these circumstances.

D The only time that COSGRIFF commits an offence of assault is when he threatens BURNELL inside his car.

34. Inspector LEPPING attends the scene of a s. 18 wounding incident (an offence contrary to the Offences Against the Person Act 1861) outside a nightclub. The victim has received several serious stab injuries and witnesses inform Inspector LEPPING that these were caused with a knife and that the offender walked away from the scene several minutes prior to the officer's arrival. Inspector LEPPING reasonably believes that the offender responsible for the offence and carrying the knife is in the locality and that it would be expedient to find the knife to authorise stop and search powers under s. 60 of the Criminal Justice and Public Order Act 1994.

Can Inspector LEPPING authorise the use of this power?

A Yes, but as soon as practicable, Inspector LEPPING must inform an officer of the rank of super-intendent that he has done so.

B No, as this is a single incident and the powers under the Act are designed to deal with a number of incidents rather than just one.

C Yes, but the power can only be exercised for a maximum time period of four hours from the time the authorisation is given.

D No, as powers under this section of the Act can only be authorised by an officer of the rank of superintendent or above.

35. PC GUILD is being investigated by a professional standards unit. A number of issues have been raised and are being looked into by Inspector BARKES who is considering PC GUILD's behaviour as potential grounds for a charge of misconduct in a public office (contrary to common law).

Considering that offence, which of the comments below is correct?

A One incident being investigated involves an alleged omission by PC GUILD. This would not be an offence of misconduct in a public office as it is a conduct offence and cannot be committed by omission.

B One incident related to a purely personal matter arising while PC GUILD was off duty. Such behaviour can amount to an offence of misconduct in a public office.

C One incident relates to an accidental action by PC GUILD; this could still amount to an offence of misconduct in a public office.

D If PC GUILD were convicted of the offence there is no limit on the sentence of imprisonment that could be passed.

36. LAKE, McNAB and NISBET are part of a group of 20 people protesting outside their local council offices over a rise in council tax. Feelings start to run high and the whole group chant, '*You're gonna get your fuckin' heads kicked in!*' towards the council offices. LAKE picks up a stone and throws it at the council offices; the stone falls short of its target. Several minutes later, the group are approached by STRACHAN, a council official, who tries to calm them down. McNAB and NISBET physically attack STRACHAN, punching him in the face. STRACHAN defends himself and punches NISBET in the face.

Who of the below would be guilty of the offence of riot (contrary to s. 1 of the Public Order Act 1986)?

A Only McNAB and NISBET.

B LAKE, McNAB and NISBET.

C LAKE, McNAB, NISBET and STRACHAN.

D LAKE, McNAB, NISBET, STRACHAN and all of the other protesters.

37. MIDDLETON (aged 16 years) is arrested for assault and his father is called to the police station to act as an appropriate adult. On arrival at the police station, MIDDLETON's father is shown into the custody area and in the presence of his son, he is informed of the circumstances of his son's arrest and his son is given his rights (again). MIDDLETON requests a solicitor and his father agrees with this request. At this point, MIDDLETON's father says, '*I know a little bit about the law myself, so I'd like to have a look at my son's custody record please*'.

Which of the statements below is correct with regard to Mr MIDDLETON's entitlement to examine his son's custody record?

A Other than police officers, the only other person permitted to examine MIDDLETON's custody record would be his solicitor.

B MIDDLETON's father must be permitted to consult his son's custody record as soon as practicable and at any other time while his son is detained.

C MIDDLETON's father can examine his son's custody record when he first arrives at the police station, but will not be permitted to do so at any other time.

D If an officer of the rank of inspector or above authorises it, MIDDLETON's father can consult his son's custody record.

38. EASTWOOD is charged with a s. 47 assault and is released on bail with the conditions that she is not to contact the victim of the offence and that she provide a surety. COOKE acts as EASTWOOD's surety. Three days after EASTWOOD's release, COOKE telephones PC SNEEDEN (the officer in the case) and informs him that EASTWOOD is unlikely to surrender to custody and, for that reason, he wishes to be relieved of his obligations as a surety.

Considering the powers under s. 7 of the Bail Act 1976, which of the statements below is correct?

A PC SNEEDEN can arrest EASTWOOD because of the information provided to him by COOKE.
B The only reason that will allow PC SNEEDEN to arrest EASTWOOD is if he has reasonable grounds to believe EASTWOOD will break any of her bail conditions.
C PC SNEEDEN will not be able to arrest EASTWOOD because the notification by COOKE was not made in writing.
D The only reason that will allow PC SNEEDEN to arrest EASTWOOD is if he has reasonable grounds for believing that EASTWOOD is not likely to surrender to custody.

39. BURDOCK works in a small shop owned by CAIN. The shop has been subject to several criminal damage offences where the front window to the shop has been smashed. As a result, CAIN has security grilles fitted to the shop front. CAIN tells BURDOCK that he is not entirely convinced the grilles are good quality and that *they should really be put to the test*. BURDOCK thinks that CAIN wants him to test the strength of the grilles and later that evening after the shop has closed BURDOCK returns to the shop with a hacksaw and a large hammer. Believing that CAIN has given him his permission, BURDOCK attacks the security grilles with both items and although he damages the grilles he does not manage to break them. The attack causes £1,000.00 worth of damage to the grilles. A passing police patrol is called to the scene because of the noise that BURDOCK has been making. When the officers arrive BURDOCK tells them that he *is only doing his job*.

With regard to the offence of criminal damage (contrary to s. 1(1) of the Criminal Damage Act 1971), which of the following statements is correct?

A BURDOCK's actions were not carried out in order to protect the property therefore he has no lawful excuse to behave in this way and has committed the offence.
B Damage that exceeds £500.00 cannot be justified on the grounds of permission; BURDOCK has committed the offence.
C BURDOCK believed his actions were carried out with the permission of the owner of the property and so he has a lawful excuse to commit criminal damage.
D BURDOCK's belief that he has the permission of CAIN is immaterial; he has committed the offence.

40. ARKLEY is considering holding a public procession to protest about the behaviour of the management of a local factory who have sacked several workers for misconduct. ARKLEY wishes the protest to pass by the factory and also to pass by the houses of several members of the factory management team. He wants to know about conditions that can be imposed on the conduct of the procession and visits his local police station to speak to PS SUDIN for information about his concerns.

With regard to the law relating to public processions (Public Order Act 1986), which of the comments below is true?

A PS SUDIN should inform ARKLEY that the only person who can impose conditions on a public procession is the chief officer of police.

B ARKLEY should be informed that conditions can be imposed on a public procession prior to the procession taking place; these conditions are provided by an officer of the rank of superintendent or above.

C PS SUDIN should inform ARKLEY that if the public procession is authorised then once the procession has started the most senior ranking officer present at the scene of the procession may impose conditions.

D ARKLEY should be told that conditions can be imposed both before and during the procession but this must always be imposed by an officer not below the rank of inspector.

41. SHEWARD is a member of a gang who are responsible for a series of robberies. SHEWARD is arrested at the scene of the gang's latest robbery but the other members of the gang manage to escape. SHEWARD is taken to a designated police station where he requests that his friend, BUCKLER, is informed of his arrest. The arresting officer, DC DOVEY, believes that BUCKLER is the person who handles the stolen goods from the robberies and that informing BUCKLER of SHEWARD's arrest would hinder the recovery of property from the robberies. DC DOVEY wishes to delay SHEWARD's exercise of this right.

Which of the statements below is correct?

A The delay can be authorised by an inspector. The maximum period of the delay is 36 hours.

B The delay can be authorised by an inspector. The maximum period of the delay is 48 hours.

C The delay must be authorised by a superintendent. The maximum period of the delay is 36 hours.

D The delay must be authorised by a superintendent. The maximum period of the delay is 48 hours.

42. TOLDAN and BRIGHOUSE work in the same factory. BRIGHOUSE is accused of theft in the factory and TOLDAN, who does not like BRIGHOUSE, provides a witness statement on an MG9 (as per the Criminal Justice Act 1967) to the police about the incident. In the statement TOLDAN makes several material statements regarding the theft which he knows are false. BRIGHOUSE is dismissed from the factory and takes his employers to an industrial tribunal where TOLDAN gives sworn evidence against BRIGHOUSE and, once again, TOLDAN gives material false evidence about the incident to the tribunal. BRIGHOUSE is later prosecuted for the theft in the magistrates' court and when TOLDAN is giving sworn evidence as a witness he again lies about material facts to the court.

At what stage, if at all, does TOLDAN first commit an offence of perjury (contrary to s. 11 of the Perjury Act 1911)?

A When he makes several false statements in the MG9.
B When he provides false sworn evidence at the industrial tribunal.
C When he provides false sworn evidence in the magistrates' court.
D At no stage has TOLDAN committed the offence of perjury.

43. KILLIP is arrested and charged with an offence of being in charge of a mechanically propelled vehicle when unfit through drink or drugs (contrary to s. 4(2) of the Road Traffic Act 1988). At court, KILLIP maintains that there was no likelihood of him driving his vehicle because at the material time the vehicle (a Ford Fiesta) had received substantial damage to the front offside wheel meaning that it could not actually be driven and, in addition, KILLIP had a broken left wrist meaning he was incapable of actually driving the vehicle.

Will the damage to the vehicle or the injury to KILLIP automatically mean that he will be successful in avoiding a conviction for the offence?

A No, as there is no defence to the offence of being in charge of a mechanically propelled vehicle whilst unfit through drink or drugs.
B Yes, as the court must take into account the condition of the vehicle at the time of the offence.
C No, in determining whether KILLIP was likely to drive the vehicle a court may disregard any injury to him or damage to his vehicle.
D Yes, as an injury that prevents the defendant from driving will preclude a conviction under s. 4(2) of the Act.

44. HUNT, PLANT and FINCH are involved in people trafficking. HUNT arranges for STEINER (a German national) to arrive in the United Kingdom and intends to use her to make money in the United Kingdom from prostitution. STEINER arrives in the United Kingdom at Dover and is met by HUNT who takes her to meet PLANT. PLANT is totally aware of where STEINER has come from and what will happen to STEINER and drives her to a brothel in Birmingham which is run by FINCH who is also aware of STEINER's origins. In Birmingham STEINER is forced into prostitution. STEINER proves popular with the customers of the brothel and hearing about this popularity, FINCH decides that he will send her to a better quality brothel in France to make even more money from her exploitation. FINCH arranges for STEINER to be sent to Paris to do so.

Considering the offence of people trafficking (contrary to s. 4 of the Asylum and Immigration (Treatment of Claimants etc.) Act 2004, which of the following statements is correct?

- **A** The offence has not been committed as STEINER is from Germany (a European Economic Community country).
- **B** HUNT, PLANT and FINCH all commit the offence.
- **C** Only HUNT and PLANT commit the offence.
- **D** Only HUNT commits the offence.

45. PC GRANT is on uniform foot patrol when he stops a car owned and driven by FRANKLIN. The officer can see a number of firearms in the back of FRANKLIN's vehicle which FRANKLIN describes as 'shotguns'.

Which of the firearms in the back of FRANKLIN's car would be classed as a 'shotgun' under s. 1(3)(a) of the Firearms Act 1968 (as amended by the Firearms Amendment Act 1988)?

- **A** A rifle-barrelled gun with a barrel measuring 36 inches in length.
- **B** A smooth-bore gun with a barrel measuring 20 inches in length.
- **C** A rifle-barrelled gun with a barrel measuring 26 inches in length.
- **D** A smooth-bore gun with a barrel measuring 25 inches in length.

46. SKIDMORE (aged 18 years) has been charged with an offence of burglary and bailed to appear at a magistrates' court. On the day SKIDMORE is due to appear at the magistrates' court, he fails to appear.

Which of the following statements is correct in relation to the options the magistrates' court has in such a situation?

- **A** As SKIDMORE is under 21 years of age, the court cannot proceed in his absence.
- **B** As SKIDMORE is 18 years of age, the court may proceed in his absence unless it appears to the court that it would be contrary to the interests of justice to do so.
- **C** The court may proceed in SKIDMORE's absence but only if the court enquires into the reasons for SKIDMORE's failure to appear.
- **D** If the court proceeds and imposes a custodial sentence on SKIDMORE, SKIDMORE must be brought before the court before commencing the custodial sentence.

47. JONES is arrested for a series of complicated fraud-related offences. During the course of the day he is interviewed about the offences by PCs NIGHTINGALE and SPALTON. The last interview concludes at 10.30 pm and at this stage JONES's eight-hour rest period begins. One hour into JONES's rest period (at 11.30 pm), JONES requests that he be interviewed as he wishes to confess to the offences.

Which of the statements below is correct with regard to this situation?

A JONES's rest period can only be interrupted if there are reasonable grounds for believing that a failure to interrupt it would involve a risk of harm to people or serious loss of, or damage to, property.

B JONES's rest period can be interrupted in these circumstances but such an interruption will not require a fresh rest period to be allowed.

C The eight-hour rest period cannot be interrupted at the request of JONES.

D JONES's rest period can only be interrupted if an officer of the rank of inspector or above authorises it.

48. PS HOWARD is in charge of a team of officers investigating a spate of thefts from motor vehicles where high value computer equipment has been stolen from delivery vans carrying out deliveries in Farrow Road. PS HOWARD decides to park a van in Farrow Road and leave the back door open exposing several empty computer boxes (as per the modus operandi of the previous crimes). She intends to observe the van and tempt would-be offenders into taking the empty boxes and then arrest them. The operation is set up and SEARS (who is long-term unemployed) passes the van and takes one of the boxes. He is arrested and charged with the theft but states that he is not guilty as he was entrapped by the police.

Which of the statements below is correct with regard to the activity carried out by PS HOWARD.

A It is not acceptable for the police to lure citizens into committing acts that are against the law and then prosecute them for doing so and it is likely proceedings against SEARS will be discontinued.

B PS HOWARD's operation did no more than give SEARS the unexceptional opportunity to commit a crime and the charge of theft from a motor vehicle would not be affected.

C Entrapment can only occur when an undercover officer induces or pressurises a defendant into committing an offence. Therefore, PS HOWARD's operation would be unaffected by the claim.

D SEARS' personal circumstances (e.g. his vulnerability and experience) will not be considered when deciding if he has been entrapped.

49. PC GRAINGER is on uniform foot patrol when she hears a radio message relating to a blue Ford Fiesta driven by a white male who is wearing a bright yellow and red baseball cap and who was seen acting suspiciously at the rear of an electrical goods store. Minutes later, PC GRAINGER sees a blue Ford Fiesta parked on the driveway of a dwelling. Leaning against the driver's door is a white male wearing a bright yellow and red baseball cap. PC GRAINGER has reasonable suspicion that the car and the white male are the same as those seen in suspicious circumstances minutes earlier and that she will find stolen or prohibited articles on the man. She is considering exercising her powers under s. 1 of the Police and Criminal Evidence Act 1984.

Can PC GRAINGER use her power to stop and search (under s. 1 of the Police and Criminal Evidence Act 1984)?

A Yes, but only if she has reasonable grounds for believing he does not reside in the dwelling and that he is there without the express or implied permission of a person who resides in the dwelling.

B No, as the male is on land occupied or used with a dwelling, PC GRAINGER cannot exercise her power to search in any circumstances.

C Yes, this power can be exercised regardless of where the person to be searched is located at the time the search is to be carried out.

D No, as the power can only be exercised if PC GRAINGER reasonably believes that she will find stolen or prohibited articles.

50. LYALL has been charged with an offence of kidnapping and has been refused bail. Under s. 40 of the Police and Criminal Evidence Act 1984, LYALL will still have to have his detention reviewed.

Which of the statements below is correct with regard to that review?

A The custody officer will carry out the review within six hours of the last decision to refuse bail.

B An officer of the rank of inspector or above will carry out the review within six hours of the last decision to refuse bail.

C The custody officer will carry out the review within nine hours of the last decision to refuse bail.

D An officer of the rank of inspector or above will carry out the review within nine hours of the last decision to refuse bail.

51. LEWIS is on holiday in France and while looking at jewellery in a shop in Paris, he steals a Rolex watch (committing an offence under French law in the process). He returns to England and while he is having a drink in his local pub and wearing the watch, he boasts about the theft. CROWE overhears LEWIS and offers LEWIS £200 for the watch which is worth at least £3,000. LEWIS agrees and the exchange takes place. CROWE takes the watch and the following day he gives it to THACKERY as a birthday present. THACKERY has no idea that the watch has been stolen.

Considering the offence of handling stolen goods (contrary to s. 22 of the Theft Act 1968) and the term 'stolen goods' (as per s. 24 of the Theft Act 1968), which of the following comments is correct?

A No offence of handling has taken place as the theft occurred in France and not in England or Wales.

B When CROWE gives the watch to THACKERY, it ceases to be stolen goods for the purposes of the offence of handling stolen goods.

C In this situation the offence of handling stolen goods has been committed but only LEWIS and CROWE are guilty.

D The £200 cash in the hands of LEWIS would not be considered 'stolen goods'.

52. On 1 December 2008, a number of Statutory Instruments brought into effect a new performance, conduct and complaints framework. The conduct procedures are supported by a code of ethics—the Standards of Professional Behaviour—which provide the yard-stick by which the conduct of police officers is to be judged.

With regard to the above Standards, which of the following comments is correct?

A The Standards of Professional Behaviour apply to police officers of all ranks from chief constable to constable.

B The Standards of Professional Behaviour do not apply to special constables.

C The Standards of Professional Behaviour apply to all police officers between the rank of constable and superintendent.

D The Standards of Behaviour do not apply to officers who are subject to suspension.

53. PC ROCCO is investigating an offence of robbery and has good evidence that LUMB is responsible for the offence. PC ROCCO visits LUMB's home address to arrest him for the offence and when the officer arrives she sees LUMB in his front garden cutting the lawn. LUMB sees PC ROCCO and states, *'I know exactly why you are here, its about that robbery I committed isn't it?'* PC ROCCO arrests and cautions LUMB for the offence. Later on and back at the police station, PC ROCCO is considering her interview plan and where, if at all, LUMB's comment to her, should fit in during her interview with LUMB.

With regard to significant statements, which of the comments below is correct?

A LUMB's comment is a significant statement and should be put to LUMB at the start of the interview.

B LUMB's comment is not a significant statement as it was not made when PC ROCCO related the circumstances of the arrest to the custody officer.

C LUMB's comment is a significant statement and should be put to LUMB at the end of the interview in respect of the robbery offence.

D LUMB's comment is not a significant statement as it was made prior to his arrest.

54. JOHNSON (aged 15 years) was given a final warning three years ago in respect of a minor offence of theft. Today, JOHNSON is arrested by PC FRANKEL for another minor offence of theft where there is ample evidence to provide a realistic prospect of conviction. PC FRANKEL interviews JOHNSON in the presence of an appropriate adult and in the interview, JOHNSON makes a full and frank confession to the offence. PC FRANKEL is satisfied that it would not be in the public interest to prosecute JOHNSON as the offence is not in any way serious.

In such circumstances, could JOHNSON be given another final warning (under the Crime and Disorder Act 1998)?

A No, final warnings can only be given on one occasion.

B Yes, as JOHNSON's previous final warning was given to him more than two years ago.

C No, as the offence committed by JOHNSON was of the same nature as the previous offence he received a final warning for.

D Yes, as long as PC FRANKEL liaises with the Crown Prosecution Service who agree to the second final warning being given.

55. ALDINGTON is at his home address when HORROBIN, a registered charity collector on behalf of the blind, calls at his house. HORROBIN wants to find out what ALDINGTON has done with some money he collected after running a sponsored half-marathon (ALDINGTON has actually spent the money). HORROBIN manages to get into ALDINGTON's hallway and the two have a brief argument before HORROBIN leaves. After HORROBIN has left, ALDINGTON notices that he has dropped his identification card in his hallway. The card identifies the holder as a registered charity collector for the blind. ALDINGTON thinks that the identification card will assist a friend of his, GIFFORD, to commit offences of fraud by false representation (contrary to s. 2 of the Fraud Act 2006) and picks the card up. He telephones GIFFORD and offers him the identification card, an offer GIFFORD accepts. ALDINGTON later leaves his house with the identification card in his pocket with a view to passing it on to GIFFORD.

Considering the offence of possession or control of articles for use in frauds (contrary to s. 6 of the Fraud Act 2006) only, at what point, if at all, does ALDINGTON first commit the offence?

A When he initially picks the card up in his hallway.
B When he telephones GIFFORD and offers him the card.
C When he leaves his house with the card in his possession.
D The offence is not committed in these circumstances.

56. PCs KING and OLDER are called to a disturbance in the street where two women, LERWICK and DRAY, are apparently behaving in a very strange manner. The officers arrive at the scene and see both women behaving in a highly erratic manner. The officers believe that both women are suffering from a mental disorder and are in immediate need of care and so use their powers under the Mental Health Act 1983 to detain the women and take them to a place of safety. Both women are placed in the officers' police vehicle and are transported to a residential care home. En route, LERWICK manages to escape from the vehicle and although PC KING chases her, she escapes. DRAY is taken to the residential home by the officers who, four hours later, receive a radio message that DRAY has escaped from the home. Two hours later the officers see both women in the same place they were originally taken from.

With regard to the powers to retake escaped patients under the Mental Health Act 1983, which of the statements below is correct?

A Only LERWICK can be retaken under the powers of the Act.
B Only DRAY can be retaken under the powers of the Act.
C Both LERWICK and DRAY can be retaken under the powers of the Act.
D Neither woman can be retaken as the initial action by the officers taking LERWICK and DRAY into custody should not have been done without first speaking to a medical professional.

57. PARSON and MILLER had a sexual relationship 15 years ago but split up from each other after six months together. The two never married. MILLER gave birth to a boy nine months after the split and PARSON believes himself to be the father of the child who is now 13 years old. PARSON has tried to contact the boy on several occasions but has never been successful and has always been told by MILLER that he is not the father of the child (this is true). PARSON is aware of the school that the child attends and that MILLER always picks the child up outside the school. He waits outside the school and when the child leaves the school he approaches the child, tells him that he is his father and asks him to accompany him to a McDonald's restaurant to have a chat. The child agrees and they visit the restaurant. MILLER arrives at the school, finds out what has gone on and calls the police.

In relation to the offence of child abduction (contrary to s. 2 of the Child Abduction Act 1984) only, which of the following statements is correct?

A PARSON has committed the offence and has no defence as he is not actually the father of the child.
B The offence has not been committed as the child consented to go with PARSON and no force was used on the child.
C PARSON has committed the offence in these circumstances but would have a defence if he can prove that he believed, on reasonable grounds, that he was the child's father.
D The offence has not been committed as PARSON has not taken or sent the child out of the United Kingdom.

58. DICKINSON is a well-known handler of stolen goods. DC EDGLEY arrests him in connection with a burglary in which a warehouse was broken into and 200 microwave ovens were stolen. Along with DICKINSON's home address, DC EDGLEY wishes to search a house DICKINSON owns and occupies one night a week, and also a 'lock-up' garage that DC EDGLEY suspects DICKINSON controls. DC EDGLEY suspects that GARNER owns the lock-up garage because he saw him standing outside the lock-up garage three times in the one week prior to his arrest.

Considering the powers to search under s. 18 of the Police and Criminal Evidence Act 1984 only, which of the statements below is correct?

A DC EDGLEY may only search DICKINSON's home address.
B DC EDGLEY may only search DICKINSON's home address and the house owned and occupied by DICKINSON.
C DC EDGLEY may search all three premises if he has reasonable grounds to suspect that there is evidence relating to the handling offence or some other offence similar to the handling offence in the premises.
D DC EDGLEY may search all three premises, as the only requirement to authorise a s. 18 search is that DICKINSON is in custody and under arrest for an indictable offence.

59. IRVING has been arrested for causing grievous bodily harm (contrary to s. 18 of the Offences Against the Person Act 1861) and has been brought into the custody block of a designated police station. The custody officer, PS PANNEL notices several deep lacerations to IRVING's hands and calls a health-care professional to examine and treat IRVING's injuries. A health-care professional attends the station and examines IRVING's injuries. The health-care professional gives PS PANNEL some guidance on the continuing care of IRVING and also tells PS PANNEL that he believes that the cause of the injuries to IRVING's hands are due to him being involved in the s. 18 wounding offence.

With regard to the medical record/custody record, which of the following statements is correct?

A All information about the injuries to IRVING, including the health-care professional's opinion as to their cause, must be recorded in the custody record.

B The custody officer need not record any information about the guidance or opinion as to the cause of the injuries given by the health-care professional.

C Information regarding the cause of IRVING's injuries can be excluded from the custody record with the authorisation of an officer of inspector rank or above.

D Information about the cause of the injury to IRVING does not have to be recorded on the custody record if it appears capable of providing evidence of the offence.

60. KNULLER (a female), WADE and COOPER (both males) are part of a group of friends drinking in a busy pub on a Friday evening. The three are teasing NOVAK, a male member of the bar staff of the pub, about his sexuality. Intending NOVAK to be distressed KNULLER exposes her breasts to him and shouts *'fancy a go on these!'* WADE, also intending NOVAK to be distressed, exposes his penis and shouts *'perhaps he'd rather have a go at this!'* COOPER, also intending to cause distress to NOVAK, exposes his buttocks and shouts *'or maybe this?'*

Who, if anyone, commits the offence of exposure (contrary to s. 66 of the Sexual Offences Act 2003)?

A All three commit the offence.

B Only WADE and COOPER commit the offence.

C Only KNULLER and WADE commit the offence.

D Only WADE commits the offence.

61. LOPEZ is charged with an offence of criminal damage (to the value of £500) and enters a plea of 'guilty' to the charge at magistrates' court.

In relation to the duties created by the Criminal Procedure and Investigations Act 1996, which of the following statements is correct?

A In such a case the prosecution must make primary or initial disclosure only.

B The rules of disclosure do not apply to cases where a defendant pleads guilty at magistrates' court.

C The plea and court are immaterial; the prosecution must make primary or initial disclosure followed by a continual duty to disclose throughout the duration of the case.

D It does not matter what court the charge is heard in, disclosure is not necessary when the defendant pleads 'guilty' to a charge.

62. HARKER is an animal rights activist who is determined to close down Jesson Research, a laboratory carrying out medical experiments on animals. On one occasion, HARKER sends a threatening letter to RUMBOLD, who works for a company supplying goods to Jesson Research. On another occasion, HARKER sends a threatening e-mail to TAYLOR, who works for a separate company who also supplies goods to Jesson Research. HARKER intends that his actions will persuade the companies that RUMBOLD and TAYLOR work for, not to supply Jesson Research.

Considering the offence of harassment (contrary to ss. 1 and 2 of the Protection from Harassment Act 1997), which of the statements below is correct?

A HARKER does not commit the offence because his conduct is aimed at two individuals rather than one person.

B As the word 'person' in the Act does not include companies or corporate bodies, Jesson Research could not apply for an injunction.

C HARKER has committed the offence in these circumstances.

D This would not amount to an offence as HARKER has not satisfied the requirement of pursuing a 'course of conduct'.

63. TRAVIS (aged 12 years) has been convicted of an offence of theft in the youth court. TRAVIS's guardian, MELLOW, was in the court at the time TRAVIS was convicted along with TRAVIS's biological parents, Amanda TRAVIS (the mother) and Martin GORTON (the father). TRAVIS's mother and father never married and have been separated for six years.

Who can such a parenting order be made against?

A Either MELLOW, Amanda TRAVIS or Martin GORTON.

B Either Amanda TRAVIS or Martin GORTON.

C Either MELLOW or Amanda TRAVIS.

D MELLOW only.

64. TOLLY is employed to drive a dumper truck. He predominantly drives the dumper truck on two building sites but has to travel 500 metres on a road that separates the two sites at least 12 times a day. On a wet day TOLLY travels between the building sites and on his way drives through puddles of water at the side of the road, deliberately spraying water from the puddles onto pedestrians. He drives between the building sites three times in a 30-minute period, splashing pedestrians with water from the puddles each time. BULL, one of the pedestrians, calls the police and PC WALSH (an officer in uniform) attends the scene. When the officer arrives, several other pedestrians who had been splashed by TOLLY on the previous two occasions approach the officer.

Considering the offence of careless and inconsiderate driving (contrary to s. 3 of the Road Traffic Act 1988) and the provisions of s. 59 of the Police Reform Act 2002, which of the comments below is correct?

A PC WALSH has the power to seize and remove the dumper truck.
B The offence under s. 3 has not been committed as a dumper truck is a mechanically propelled vehicle and s. 3 of the Road Traffic Act 1988 only applies to motor vehicles.
C Evidence of the earlier incidents within the 30-minute period could not be used to support a charge of careless and inconsiderate driving against TOLLY.
D Spraying pedestrians with water from a puddle would not be classed as careless or inconsiderate driving.

65. HOLTHAM walks into a bank and towards a till operated by DARNLEY. Holding his stiffened fingers beneath his coat to appear like a firearm, he tells DARNLEY she will be shot if she does not hand over the takings. DARNLEY does so and HOLTHAM escapes. HOLTHAM later uses the cash from the bank robbery to purchase a real firearm and uses the real firearm to assist him to commit an offence of rape. Later, HOLTHAM is cleaning the firearm in his house when the police burst in and arrest him for an unrelated offence of causing grievous bodily harm with intent (contrary to s. 18 of the Offences Against the Person Act 1861).

At what point, if at all, does HOLTHAM first commit the offence of possessing a firearm while committing or being arrested for a Schedule 1 offence (contrary to s. 17(2) of the Firearms Act 1968)?

A When he robs the bank.
B When he commits the rape.
C When he is arrested for the offence of s. 18 wounding.
D HOLTHAM does not commit the offence in these circumstances.

66. EBURY is the caretaker of a secondary school and is provided with a caretaker's house and garden by the school. EBURY's house is used solely as his dwelling. GLENN and HAYWARD visit EBURY at his home and the three have a barbeque in EBURY's garden. GLENN is in possession of a dagger and HAYWARD is in possession of a closed folding pocket knife; the cutting edge of the pocket knife is 3 inches long.

    Who, if anyone, commits an offence under s. 139A(1) of the Criminal Justice Act 1988 (having a bladed or sharply pointed article on school premises)?

    A HAYWARD only.
    B GLENN only.
    C HAYWARD and GLENN.
    D No offence is committed by either of the above.

67. POTTER is driving her Vauxhall Astra motor vehicle along a road; sitting in the passenger seat of the vehicle is POTTER's friend GUNNER. POTTER pulls up outside a cash-point and applies the handbrake of the vehicle but leaves the engine of the Astra running. POTTER asks GUNNER to 'mind the car' while she quickly visits the cash-point. GUNNER agrees to do so.

    Considering only the offence of 'quitting' (contrary to reg. 107 of the Road Vehicles (Construction and Use) Regulations 1986), which of the following comments is true?

    A The offence of 'quitting' has been committed by POTTER is these circumstances.
    B GUNNER must be in the driver's seat of the Astra otherwise the offence has been committed by POTTER.
    C If GUNNER has a driving licence to drive the Astra then no offence has been committed.
    D The offence has not been committed by POTTER as the brake has been set on the vehicle.

68. One of the central elements of the offence of burglary under s. 9(1)(a) of the Theft Act 1968 is the intention of the offender at the time of entry.

    Consider that all of the other elements of the offence are present, in which one of the following scenarios has an offence of s. 9(1)(a) burglary been committed?

    A LEWIS enters a house with the intention of committing criminal damage (contrary to s. 1(1) of the Criminal Damage Act 1971) to property inside the house.
    B DE SOUZA enters a house with the intention of causing actual bodily harm (contrary to s. 47 of the Offences Against the Person Act 1861) to a person inside the house.
    C TRENCH enters a house with the intention of raping (contrary to s. 1 of the Sexual Offences Act 2003) a person inside the house.
    D SMITH enters a house with the intention of kidnapping (contrary to common law) a person inside the house.

69. CUNNINGHAM (aged 13 years) has been arrested for an offence of robbery. The custody officer, PS ALEXANDER, is considering the issue of bail for CUNNINGHAM and in particular the imposition of conditions on CUNNINGHAM to ensure that he surrenders to custody at the appointed time at court. PS ALEXANDER is contemplating a surety for CUNNINGHAM which would be provided by CUN-NINGHAM's father.

Which of the following statements is true with regard to such a condition of bail?

A A surety or security cannot be imposed as a condition of bail on a person under the age of 17.

B A surety condition could be imposed on CUNNINGHAM but it cannot be provided by a relative such as CUNNINGHAM's father.

C A surety can only be imposed on CUNNINGHAM if he will be under the age of 14 when he actually appears in court.

D CUNNINGHAM's father can provide a surety for his son but this cannot exceed the sum of £50.00.

70. MITCHAM has a grudge against a work colleague, JAMIL. MITCHAM buys some 'joke' laxative powder and places the powder into JAMIL's mug of tea in the works canteen. MITCHAM does not intend to injure JAMIL: he just wants to annoy him by forcing him to go to the toilet. JAMIL drinks his tea but the laxative powder has no effect.

Does MITCHAM commit the offence of poisoning with intent (contrary to s. 24 of the Offences Against the Person Act 1861)?

A No, MITCHAM does not commit an offence as the laxative did not affect JAMIL.

B Yes, MITCHAM commits the offence because he intended to annoy JAMIL.

C No, MITCHAM does not commit the offence as he did not intend to injure JAMIL.

D Yes, MITCHAM commits the offence which is punishable with 10 years' imprisonment.

71. FERRIS is sitting outside a pub and has drunk several large vodka drinks (enough to mean that if he drove he would exceed the prescribed limit). RIDING approaches FERRIS and producing a handgun he states, *'I've been looking for you, time for you to die!'* FERRIS believes that RIDING is going to kill him and pushing past RIDING he quickly gets into his car and drives off the pub car park and onto the road. He does so at great speed and swerves violently down the road, causing several cars to veer off the road to avoid colliding with him. Once FERRIS is clear of the pub and the road it is situated in, he pulls over and parks his car. At this point PCs GARNER and BURR arrive and speak to FERRIS.

In respect of the defence of duress of circumstances, which of the following comments is correct?

A Duress of circumstances is not a defence that is applicable to road traffic law.

B FERRIS could use the defence in answer to charges of careless and inconsiderate driving (contrary to s. 3 of the Road Traffic Act 1988) and also to driving a motor vehicle whilst over the prescribed limit (contrary to s. 5(1)(a) of the Road Traffic Act 1988).

C FERRIS could use the defence in answer to a charge of careless and inconsiderate driving (contrary to s. 3 of the Road Traffic Act 1988) but not to driving a motor vehicle whilst over the prescribed limit (contrary to s. 5(1)(a) of the Road Traffic Act 1988).

D FERRIS could use the defence in answer to a charge of driving a motor vehicle whilst over the prescribed limit (contrary to s. 5(1)(a) of the Road Traffic Act 1988) but not to careless and inconsiderate driving (contrary to s. 3 of the Road Traffic Act 1988).

72. EVAN is arrested for an offence of murder. She is interviewed and during the interview she confesses to the offence. EVAN is charged with murder and the case goes to trial, where EVAN pleads not guilty to the offence, alleging that her confession was obtained by oppression and in circumstances that would render it unreliable.

Which of the statements below is correct?

A EVAN'S 'confession' evidence can only be excluded under s. 76 of the Police and Criminal Evidence Act 1984.

B The only way evidence can be excluded during the trial is under ss. 76 and 78 of the Police and Criminal Evidence Act.

C EVAN's 'confession' falls into the category of evidence known as 'hearsay' evidence.

D Once the issue of oppression and/or unreliability is raised it is for the defence to prove that the confession was obtained in such circumstances.

73. HEATHCOTE is a racist and has a particular dislike of people from the Pakistani community. He attends a designated football match in a town where there is a large Pakistani community and sits with 'visiting' supporters. During the match he stands up and shouts towards a group of nearby 'home' supporters: 'You're just a town full of Pakis'. HEATHCOTE repeats the chant half a dozen times but nobody else joins in.

Would HEATHCOTE commit an offence of misbehaviour at a designated football match (contrary to s. 3 of the Football (Offences) Act 1991)?

A Yes, the offence is committed the first time HEATHCOTE shouts at the 'home' supporters.
B No, one person cannot commit this offence; it must be done in concert with one or more others.
C Yes, but the offence is only committed when HEATHCOTE repeats the chant.
D No, as the words uttered by HEATHCOTE would not be classed as 'racialist'.

74. JALOTA sues KNOTT for breach of contract which results in the civil court ordering KNOTT to pay £2,000 as compensation to JALOTA. KNOTT is aware that JALOTA has a particular fear about being locked in a confined space. KNOTT writes out a demand telling JALOTA to forget about the compensation: if she does not, she will be locked in the boot of her car the next time she goes shopping. KNOTT posts the letter but it is lost in the post and JALOTA never sees the letter.

Which of the following is true?

A KNOTT does not commit blackmail because, although he has made a demand with menaces, it is not made with a view to gain for himself or another.
B When the demand is made by way of a letter, the victim must receive it otherwise the only offence committed would be attempted blackmail.
C This is not blackmail as the Court of Appeal has held that words or conduct that would not intimidate or influence anyone to respond to the demand are not 'menaces'.
D When a blackmail demand is made by letter, the act of making the demand and the offence of blackmail are complete when the letter is posted.

75. BYTON has been going out with PARK for several months but the couple have not had sexual intercourse due to the fact that BYTON believes sex before marriage is immoral. PARK tells BYTON that he loves her and will marry her but only on the condition that she will have sexual intercourse with him. Believing that PARK will marry her, she permits him to have sexual intercourse with her (penis to vagina). PARK has no intention of marrying BYTON.

Would this activity constitute an offence of rape?

A Yes, because BYTON has been deceived into the act of sexual intercourse.
B No, because violence was not used or threatened against BYTON.
C Yes, because PARK had no intention of marrying BYTON.
D No, because BYTON consented to the act of sexual intercourse.

76. STANSBIE constantly causes problems for residents in his local neighbourhood. As a result of his behaviour, he is made subject to an anti-social behaviour order (ASBO) under s. 1 of the Crime and Disorder Act 1998.

    What will be the minimum duration period of the ASBO?

    A One year.
    B Two years.
    C Three years.
    D Four years.

77. KELLEHER and MOORE are rival market traders who both sell compact discs and DVDs on separate stalls. Intending to cause economic loss to MOORE by losing him business, KELLEHER places a sign on the front of MOORE's stall saying, *'Don't touch these goods—they are covered in acid!'*. Nobody actually takes any notice of the sign and MOORE's sales are unaffected.

    Considering the offence of contamination or interference with goods (contrary to s. 38(1) of the Public Order Act 1986) only, which of the comments below is true?

    A In these circumstances the offence is committed because KELLEHER intended to cause economic loss to MOORE by his actions.
    B KELLEHER does not commit the offence because the act was not intended to cause public alarm or anxiety or cause injury to members of the public.
    C Compact discs and DVDs are not covered by the legislation as they are not natural substances, i.e. foodstuffs.
    D As MOORE's sales were unaffected by KELLEHER's actions, the offence has not been committed.

78. GARBUT has unprotected consensual sexual intercourse with several women, without disclosing to the women that he is HIV positive. All of the women subsequently contract the HIV virus and complain to the police.

    Considering the law in relation to s. 20 of the Offences Against the Person Act 1861, which of the statements below is correct?

    A This could not amount to a s. 20 offence as GARBUT has not 'wounded' any of the women.
    B No offence could ever be committed in these circumstances as the women consented to sexual intercourse.
    C Infecting the women with the HIV virus can amount to grievous bodily harm.
    D Any prosecution for the s. 20 offence would need to prove that GARBUT intended serious or really serious harm to befall the women.

79. SWAN visits his friend, KENNETT, who lives on a farm surrounded by 30 acres of private farmland. KENNETT has an old BMW motor vehicle which he uses to race around in on his land and KENNETT tells SWAN he can drive the vehicle as fast as he likes on the farmland. SWAN gets into the BMW and races off at speed. SWAN drives off KENNETT's land and onto a road. Still driving at speed he swerves off the road and back onto KENNETT's land through a gate adjacent to the road. As he does so the car skids, collides with the gate and damages the gate. SWAN carries on driving and back at KENNETT's farmhouse he skids to a halt. As he does so the BMW hits a water-trough, damaging the water-trough in the process. The water-trough is hit with such force that it flies through the air and hits KENNETT, breaking KENNETT's left arm and leg.

At what point, if at all, has a reportable accident (as per s. 170 of the Road Traffic Act 1988) first occurred?

A Such a reportable accident has not occurred in these circumstances.

B A reportable accident first occurs when the BMW driven by SWAN hits the gate and damages the gate.

C A reportable accident first occurs when the BMW driven by SWAN hits the water-trough and damages the water-trough.

D A reportable accident first occurs when KENNETT is seriously injured by the flying water-trough.

80. PC EVERTON is on uniform patrol when she stops KOBEL, who is driving a BMW Z4 motor vehicle on a road. KOBEL gets out of the vehicle and speaks to the officer. KOBEL is somewhat unsteady on his feet and seems to be very animated in his actions. PC EVERTON forms the opinion that KOBEL has taken some kind of drug and is about to arrest KOBEL for an offence under s. 4(1) of the Road Traffic Act 1988 (driving or attempting to drive a mechanically propelled vehicle when unfit through drink or drugs) when KOBEL runs away from her and into a nearby house.

Can PC EVERTON enter the house to arrest KOBEL for an offence under s. 4 of the Road Traffic Act 1988?

A No, PC EVERTON cannot enter the house unless KOBEL has been involved in a road accident.

B Yes, PC EVERTON may enter and search the premises for the purpose of arresting KOBEL but only because she is in uniform.

C No, there is no power of entry to arrest an individual for an offence under this section of the Act.

D Yes, PC EVERTON may force entry to the house for the purpose of arresting KOBEL for an offence under s. 4 of the Road Traffic Act 1988.

81. DARCY takes a group of three friends to see a football match (the match is a designated sporting event under the Sporting Events (Control of Alcohol) Act 1985). DARCY drives the group to the football match in his own limousine that can carry eight passengers. DARCY has put a case of champagne in the limousine and during the journey HALLADAY drinks two bottles becoming drunk in the process. PC FLEMMING stops the limousine.

Who, if anyone, commits an offence relating to alcohol on other vehicles (contrary to s. 1A of the Sporting Events (Control of Alcohol) Act 1985)?

A DARCY only.

B HALLADAY only.

C DARCY and HALLADAY.

D No offence is committed under this legislation.

82. AWDEN has an argument with his neighbour, NORCROSS. NORCROSS walks away from AWDEN, into his house and then shuts his front door. AWDEN stands outside NORCROSS's house for several minutes before starting to shout abuse and threaten personal violence towards NORCROSS. As AWDEN is making these threats he is shaking his fist. Unknown to AWDEN, NORCROSS's house is empty as NORCROSS had left via the back door of his house before the threats of violence were made.

Has AWDEN committed an offence of affray (contrary to s. 3 of the Public Order Act 1986)?

A No, because there was nobody in NORCROSS's house.

B Yes, because the threats of violence are accompanied by AWDEN shaking his fist.

C No, because AWDEN does not actually use unlawful violence.

D Yes, because AWDEN's conduct would cause a person of reasonable firmness present at the scene to fear for their personal safety.

83. STATEN is on holiday at a campsite and has tried to become friendly with FERRY who is camping in a tent next to STATEN's motor home vehicle; FERRY has rejected all of STATEN's advances. STATEN decides he will rape FERRY and in order to make her more pliable he sneaks into her tent when she is out and places several crushed sleeping tablets in her water supply. FERRY returns to her tent, drinks the water and a short time later falls into a deep sleep. STATEN enters FERRY's tent, takes her out and into his motor home where he rapes her while she is asleep.

At what stage, if at all, does STATEN commit the offence under s. 63 of the Sexual Offences Act 2003 (trespass with intent to commit a relevant sexual offence)?

A When he enters FERRY's tent to put the sleeping tablets in her drink.

B When he enters FERRY's tent to take her back to his motor home vehicle.

C When he takes FERRY into his motor home vehicle and rapes her.

D The offence has not been committed in these circumstances.

84. Section 76(8) of the Police and Criminal Evidence Act 1984 gives some guidance as to what 'oppression' means.

Which of the comments below is true in relation to such 'oppression'?

A Where the Codes of Practice have been followed there can never be any 'oppression'.

B It might be possible for the defence to use evidence against officers involved in a case who have allegedly 'mistreated' suspects in other cases.

C The 'oppression' does not necessarily have to be against the person who makes the confession.

D A failure to follow the Codes of Practice will automatically lead to the exclusion of evidence on the grounds of 'oppression'.

85. QAZI is an Iraqi national who has made his way across Europe and into France. He meets PURCELL (a British citizen on holiday in France) and asks for his help to get into the United Kingdom. PURCELL agrees to help QAZI and gives QAZI his car and passport. QAZI drives through United Kingdom border controls and into the United Kingdom.

Considering the offence of assisting unlawful immigration to member states (contrary to s. 25 of the Immigration Act 1971), which of the below is true?

A PURCELL does not commit the offence because he has not acted for gain.

B The prosecution only has to show that PURCELL knew or had reasonable cause to believe that his act was facilitating the commission of a breach of immigration law.

C If PURCELL were convicted of the offence, a court could order the forfeiture of his car.

D PURCELL has not committed the offence because he was outside the United Kingdom when he helped QAZI.

86. McGOWAN breaks into a Nissan 350Z motor vehicle and drives it around his local area. He sees a friend of his, PLAYDON, walking along a street and pulls up next to him and invites him to get into the car. PLAYDON gets into the front passenger seat and McGOWAN drives the vehicle to the end of the street where the two are stopped and arrested by the police.

If PLAYDON is to be convicted of an offence of allowing himself to be carried (under s. 12 of the Theft Act 1968), what needs to be proved by the prosecution?

A Only that PLAYDON knew that the conveyance had been taken without the required consent or authority.

B Only that PLAYDON suspected the conveyance had been taken without the required consent or authority.

C That PLAYDON allowed himself to be carried in the vehicle, that he knew the conveyance had been taken without the required consent or authority, and that there was some movement of the conveyance while PLAYDON was in it.

D That PLAYDON suspected the conveyance had been taken without the required consent or authority and that there was some movement of the conveyance while PLAYDON was in it.

87. DS CABLE works on an Anti-Terrorist Unit and is informed that the Secretary of State has made an application to the court for a derogating control order to be made against JUPHAN under the Prevention of Terrorism Act 2005. DS CABLE is provided with good quality intelligence that it will be necessary to arrest and detain JUPHAN to ensure that he is available to be given notice of the order if it is made. JUPHAN is duly arrested and taken to a designated place that DS CABLE considers most appropriate as soon as practicable after his arrest.

Without the authority of a court, what is the maximum period JUPHAN can be detained in the designated place?

A JUPHAN may be detained until the end of 24 hours from the time of his arrest.
B JUPHAN may be detained until the end of 24 hours from the time of his arrival at the designated place.
C JUPHAN may be detained until the end of 48 hours from the time of his arrest.
D JUPHAN may be detained until the end of 48 hours from the time of his arrival at the designated place.

88. PC STEWART (who is appropriately trained and authorised to deliver a preliminary impairment test) is on uniform mobile patrol when he sees INNES driving his Land Rover Discovery motor vehicle in an erratic fashion. This causes PC STEWART to reasonably suspect that INNES has alcohol in his body or is under the influence of a drug and consequently the officer stops the vehicle. PC STEWART decides that he will test INNES (as per s. 6 of the Road Traffic Act 1988).

In respect of the tests that can be administered to INNES, which of the following statements is correct?

A PC STEWART could administer a preliminary impairment test to INNES at a police station specified by PC STEWART if he thinks it expedient.
B PC STEWART could administer a preliminary breath test to INNES at a police station specified by PC STEWART if he thinks it expedient.
C PC STEWART could administer a preliminary impairment test to INNES but this must be carried out at or near the place where the requirement to co-operate with the test is imposed.
D PC STEWART could administer a preliminary impairment test to INNES regardless of whether he was in uniform or not.

89. PRASAD has been arrested in connection with an offence of attempted kidnapping. The victim states that when PRASAD tried to kidnap her he was not wearing a top of any description and she managed to scratch him on the chest with her fingernails. The victim states that the scratches were deep and left four large marks on the left side of PRASAD's chest. The officer in the case, DS JACKSON, wishes to examine PRASAD under s. 54A of the Police and Criminal Evidence Act 1984 (as amended by the Anti-terrorism, Crime and Security Act 2001), to ascertain whether or not he has such marks on his chest as their presence would tend to identify him as the person involved in the commission of the offence.

Which of the following statements is correct?

A The custody officer can authorise that PRASAD be examined without his consent but this must be authorised in writing.

B PRASAD can be examined for the presence of the marks but only if he consents and an officer of the rank of inspector or above authorises the examination.

C PRASAD cannot be examined as the Act allows only for the search and/or examination of an individual to establish their identification and not for evidence in relation to the offence for which they have been arrested.

D An inspector must authorise the examination; authorisation can be given orally or in writing.

90. BRATLEN is driving her Ford Fiesta along a road when she is stopped by PC KHAN (on uniform foot patrol). The officer speaks to BRATLEN and asks her if she has insurance for the vehicle. BRATLEN replies '*I might have and I might not, but either way what are you going to do about it?*' and drives off. PC KHAN took the registration number of the vehicle and finds out BRATLEN's home address. PC KHAN visits the address and when he arrives he can see the Ford Fiesta parked in a garage adjoining BRATLEN's home address. PC KHAN suspects that BRATLEN has no insurance for the Ford Fiesta and is considering seizing the vehicle under the powers of the Road Traffic Act 1988.

Which of the following comments is correct?

A The power cannot be used as the garage that the Ford Fiesta is in is connected to a dwelling house.

B The power can be used but PC KHAN will require another officer (of any rank) to be present to witness the seizure.

C The power cannot be used as PC KHAN only suspects that BRATLEN has no insurance for the Ford Fiesta.

D The Ford Fiesta can be seized by the officer as he has reasonable grounds to suspect that BRATLEN has no insurance certificate to drive it.

91. Custody officers need to be aware of and give consideration to the rights and freedoms guaranteed under the European Convention on Human Rights when reaching a decision as to bail. The European Court has identified four grounds where refusal of bail may be justified under the Convention.

With regard to these grounds, which of the statements below is correct?

A A person can be temporarily detained where the particular gravity of the offence(s) and likely public reaction is that the release may give rise to public disorder.

B The fact that a detained person has previously been bailed and there was no interference with the course of justice has no bearing on future decisions to refuse bail on the ground of interference with the course of justice.

C The fact that the custody officer reasonably believes that the detained person will commit other offence(s) if bailed, would not provide reasonable grounds to refuse bail.

D The seriousness of the offence alone has been deemed to be sufficient reason to suppose a person may abscond and other factors, such as the background or financial status of the individual, are immaterial.

92. COOPER is arrested while attempting to place a large amount of deadly poison in a reservoir. On arrest he tells the arresting officer, DC WYRE, that he has planted a large bomb in a shopping centre and it will explode in the next three hours, killing hundreds of people. There is every reason to believe that COOPER is telling the truth and DC WYRE asks where the device has been planted. COOPER refuses to say and so DC WYRE tells him he will break his left wrist unless the information is provided. As a result, COOPER tells the officer the location of the bomb.

Considering only Article 3 (torture) of the Human Rights Convention, which of these statements is correct?

A COOPER's rights have not been breached as this is a public emergency threatening life and in such circumstances the state can derogate from its obligations under the Convention.

B DC WYRE has breached COOPER's human rights, as derogations from Article 3 are not permitted, irrespective of the prevailing circumstances.

C The United Kingdom has lodged a derogation under the Anti-terrorism, Crime and Security Act 2001 making the activity of DC WYRE lawful.

D Torture is classed as deliberate treatment leading to serious or cruel suffering; DC WYRE's actions would fall short of this.

93. AUSTIN has been sentenced to 12 years in prison for armed robbery and, while he is in transit from the court to the prison, the prison van in which he is being transported is involved in an accident. This enables AUSTIN to escape. He makes his way to CUTHBERT's house (who is a criminal associate of AUSTIN) and asks CUTHBERT to hide him from the police. CUTHBERT agrees and allows AUSTIN to stay at his house for three days. During this time, FRANCIS (another criminal associate of AUSTIN's) brings AUSTIN cash and forged identity documents in order to assist AUSTIN to escape.

Who, if anyone, commits an offence of harbouring an offender (contrary to s. 22(2) of the Criminal Justice Act 1961)?

A The offence is not committed.
B CUTHBERT only.
C FRANCIS only.
D Both CUTHBERT and FRANCIS.

94. BATESON is driving a quad bike along a road. Riding on the back of the quad bike is FARROW. As the bike approaches a junction controlled by a set of traffic lights, the lights turn from green to red against BATESON. FARROW shouts to BATESON, '*Quick, get across, we can do it!*' BATESON accelerates across the junction. While crossing the junction, the quad bike collides with a vehicle driven by GUEST and FARROW is killed as a consequence.

Which comment is true with regard to the offence of causing death by dangerous driving (contrary to s. 1 of the Road Traffic Act 1988)?

A BATESON does not commit the offence as the offence only applies to 'motor vehicles' and a quad bike would be classed as a 'mechanically propelled vehicle'.
B FARROW contributed to the cause of his death. Therefore, BATESON is not guilty as his driving must be shown to be the substantial cause of death.
C If BATESON were convicted of the offence, he would have to take an extended driving test before he could get his licence back.
D The test for whether the standard of driving by BATESON was dangerous or not is a subjective one.

95. Code C of the Codes of Practice provides advice and guidance in respect of solicitors and legal advice at police stations.

Which of the statements below is correct in respect of that advice and guidance?

A A trainee solicitor is not a 'solicitor' for the purposes of the Codes of Practice.
B If a solicitor arrives at a police station to see a suspect, the suspect must be asked whether he/she would like to see the solicitor unless the suspect has already received legal advice.
C If a solicitor is acting in such a way that the interviewing officer cannot properly put questions to a suspect then an officer not below the rank of inspector should be consulted to decide whether to exclude the solicitor.
D If an appropriate adult requests legal advice for a detained juvenile suspect but the juvenile does not wish to consult with the solicitor, the juvenile cannot be forced to speak to the solicitor.

96. PC NAWAZ arrests HOUSEMAN on suspicion of driving a motor vehicle while over the prescribed limit (contrary to s. 5(1)(a) of the Road Traffic Act 1988) as HOUSEMAN failed the preliminary roadside breath test. HOUSEMAN is brought to the police station to provide two samples of breath on the approved machine, a Lion Intoximeter, but the Intoximeter has broken down and is not available. As a consequence PC NAWAZ chooses to request that HOUSEMAN provide a specimen of urine, rather than a sample of blood, for examination.

Which of the statements below is correct?

A The prescribed limit in relation to urine is 80 milligrammes of alcohol in 100 millilitres of urine.

B The choice of what sample to provide (urine or blood) should be made by HOUSEMAN and not PC NAWAZ.

C A sample of urine should only be obtained at a hospital and not at a police station.

D HOUSEMAN should provide a specimen of urine within one hour of the requirement for its provision being made and after the provision of a previous specimen of urine.

97. Sections 21 to 24 of the Firearms Act 1968 place restrictions on the people who can possess, acquire, receive or otherwise have involvement with firearms. Section 21 deals with people who have been convicted of certain offences.

Which of the below comments is true with regard to s. 21 of the Act?

A ATKINSON was sentenced to two months' detention in a young offenders' institution for an offence of theft. Section 21 prohibits her from having a firearm or ammunition in her possession for a period of 3 years from the date of her release.

B FERRIS was sentenced to three years' imprisonment for an offence of robbery. Section 21 prohibits him from having a firearm or ammunition in his possession for life from the date of his release.

C RIGG was sentenced to two years' imprisonment for an offence of burglary. Section 21 prohibits her from having a firearm or ammunition in her possession for a period of four years from the date of her release.

D HASLER was sentenced to three months' youth custody for an offence of assault. Section 21 prohibits him from having a firearm or ammunition in his possession for a period of three years from the date of his conviction.

98. Once the *actus reus* of an offence has been proved, a causal link must then be shown between it and the relevant consequences. The causal link can be broken by a new and intervening act.

Which of the following comments is true with regard to intervening acts?

A If the medical treatment which a victim is given results in their untimely death, the treatment itself will normally be regarded as a 'new' intervening act.

B Defendants must 'take their victims as they find them'. This means that if a victim has a particular characteristic, such as a very thin skull, which makes the consequences of an act against them much more acute, that is the defendant's bad luck.

C If the victim of a serious sexual assault was injured when jumping from her assailant's car in order to escape then the assailant would not normally be responsible for the victim's injuries.

D A drug dealer who supplies drugs to another person who then kills himself by overdose will be said to have caused the death of the individual.

99. HAMPSHIRE and O'SHEA are work colleagues in a private mobile phone repair shop owned by HAMPSHIRE. HAMPSHIRE is owed £100.00 by O'SHEA who has constantly refused to pay the debt and HAMPSHIRE has run out of patience after three months of asking for the debt to be repaid. Believing he has a right in law to do so, HAMPSHIRE takes O'SHEA's Nokia mobile phone from O'SHEA's desk in payment for the debt (the Nokia mobile phone is worth £100.00). HAMPSHIRE takes the Nokia mobile phone back to his desk where he changes the unique device identifier on the Nokia mobile phone he took from O'SHEA.

Considering the offences of theft (contrary to s. 1 of the Theft Act 1968) and re-programming mobile phones (contrary to s. 1 of the Mobile Telephones (Re-programming) Act 2002), which of the comments below is correct?

A HAMPSHIRE does not commit the offence of theft but does commit the offence of re-progamming a mobile phone.

B HAMPSHIRE commits the offence of theft and the offence of re-programming a mobile phone.

C HAMPSHIRE commits the offence of theft but not the offence of re-progamming a mobile phone.

D HAMPSHIRE commits neither of the offences.

100. Section 80 of the Police and Criminal Evidence Act 1984 (as amended by the Youth Justice and Criminal Evidence Act 1999) details circumstances when a wife, husband or civil partner is compellable to give evidence against their spouse or civil partner.

In which of the following circumstances would the named person be compellable to give evidence on behalf of the prosecution against their spouse or civil partner?

A JOHN and ALAN are civil partners (by virtue of the Civil Partnership Act 2004). During an argument in the street, JOHN threatened to injure ALAN. JOHN is charged with an offence of affray (contrary to s. 3 of the Public Order Act 1986).

B JILL and PAUL are married. JILL witnesses PAUL commit an offence of assault by penetration (contrary to s. 2 of the Sexual Offences Act 2003) against a person who, at the time of the assault, was 16 years old.

C FRANK and JULIE are married. FRANK witnesses JULIE commit an offence of grievous bodily harm with intent (contrary to s. 18 of the Offences Against the Person Act 1861) against a person who, at the time of the assault, was 19 years old.

D KATE and MARY are civil partners (by virtue of the Civil Partnership Act 2004). KATE steals £3,000 from MARY's private bank account.

101. DEBNEY (who is 23 years old) has been arrested in connection with an offence of aggravated burglary (contrary to s. 10 of the Theft Act 1968) and is in custody at a designated police station waiting to be interviewed. A forensic examination of the scene of the crime resulted in a footwear impression being recovered. DC FEATHERSTONE, the officer in charge of the case, wishes to take footwear impressions from DEBNEY in connection with the investigation of the aggravated burglary. DEBNEY has not had an impression of his footwear taken in the course of the investigation of the offence.

Considering s. 61A of the Police and Criminal Evidence Act 1984 (power to take footwear impressions) and Code D of the Codes of Practice, which of the following statements is correct?

A Footwear impressions cannot be obtained without DEBNEY's consent unless he has been charged with a recordable offence or informed that he will be reported for such an offence.

B DC FEATHERSTONE may take DEBNEY's footwear impressions without his consent and use reasonable force to do so if necessary.

C DC FEATHERSTONE may take DEBNEY's footwear impressions without DEBNEY's consent if an officer of the rank of inspector or above authorises it.

D Footwear impressions can be obtained from DEBNEY with his oral consent.

102. PC FEARN approaches her tutor constable, PC JAY, and asks for some advice regarding the offences of assault and battery. PC JAY's supervisor overhears the advice given by PC JAY and realises that the officer has made a series of mistakes.

Which is the only correct comment made by PC JAY?

A *'You cannot commit an assault by omission. For a charge of assault to succeed, there must be an act by the defendant.'*

B *'You must show that the victim of an assault was actually in fear of the application of unlawful violence.'*

C *'Only the direct application of force would constitute a battery.'*

D *'A battery can only occur when there is a significant degree of physical contact and harm to the victim.'*

103. Section 81(1) of the Road Traffic Regulation Act 1984 provides the speed limit of a 'restricted road' and s. 82 of the same Act states what a 'restricted road' is for the purposes of the Act.

Considering those sections, which of the following statements is correct?

A The speed limit on a 'restricted road' is 20 mph. In England and Wales a 'restricted road' is one where there is provided on it a system of street lighting furnished by means of lamps placed not more than 100 yards apart.

B The speed limit on a 'restricted road' is 30 mph. In England and Wales a 'restricted road' is one where there is provided on it a system of street lighting furnished by means of lamps placed not more than 100 yards apart.

C The speed limit on a 'restricted road' is 20 mph. In England and Wales a 'restricted road' is one where there is provided on it a system of street lighting furnished by means of lamps placed not more than 200 yards apart.

D The speed limit on a 'restricted road' is 30 mph. In England and Wales a 'restricted road' is one where there is provided on it a system of street lighting furnished by means of lamps placed not more than 200 yards apart.

104. PANTRINI is sacked from his job as a computer programmer at High Tech Solutions Ltd. He believes that he has been unfairly dismissed and seeks revenge against his former employers. He sends an e-mail via the Internet to a local radio station stating, *'Next week a bomb will explode at High Tech Solutions—you have been warned!'* PANTRINI intends that whoever at the radio station receives the e-mail will believe the threat. However, it is received by SNOW at the radio station who does not believe the e-mail and deletes it.

Considering the offence of communicating false information (contrary to s. 52(2) of the Criminal Law Act 1977) only, which of the following comments is correct?

A A message threatening to place a bomb at High Tech Solutions Ltd sometime in the future would not represent an offence under the Act.

B PANTRINI does not commit the offence as an e-mail sent via the Internet would not be classed as a 'communication'.

C As SNOW does not believe the threat, no offence is committed.

D PANTRINI is guilty of the offence as he has sent the e-mail intending that whoever receives it should believe it.

105. ELSEGOOD has been arrested for an offence of kidnapping and has requested that RAITHBY act as his solicitor whilst he is in custody. RAITHBY has been contacted but tells the custody officer it will be at least four hours before he can attend the station. As a result, Superintendent HOBSON has authorised that ELSEGOOD's interview go ahead without a solicitor, as awaiting RAITHBY's arrival might lead to the physical harm of the kidnap victim who is still to be found. DS PEPPER and DC SPARGO go into an interview room with ELSEGOOD to ask him questions about the offence.

What is the correct action that should be taken in respect of the caution in such an interview?

A ELSEGOOD should not be cautioned in such circumstances.

B ELSEGOOD should be cautioned in the normal fashion, i.e. *'You do not have to say anything. But it may harm your defence if you do not mention when questioned something which you later rely on in Court. Anything you do say may be given in evidence.'*

C ELSEGOOD should be given the shorter and alternative caution, i.e. *'You do not have to say anything, but anything you do say may be given in evidence.'*

D ELSEGOOD should be given the special caution, i.e. *'You do not have to say anything but any refusal to answer questions could be subject to comment in later Court proceedings.'*

106. Sergeant FARRIER is on uniform patrol when he hears a report of a robbery where, after verbal threats to the victim, the only property stolen is a bright yellow mobile phone. PC HALLIGAN detains a suspect and Sergeant FARRIER makes his way to the scene. When he arrives, Sergeant FARRIER is told that the suspect was arrested after a short foot chase, having run through a nearby house to escape the police. The bright yellow mobile phone is recovered from the suspect. There is no outstanding stolen property and the suspect was in the house for a matter of seconds. PC HALLIGAN asks Sergeant FARRIER if, under the Police and Criminal Evidence Act 1984, there is a power to search the house the suspect has just run through.

Which answer should Sergeant FARRIER provide?

A   A search can be carried out under s. 18 of PACE, provided an inspector is informed of the search as soon as practicable after it is made.

B   A search can be carried out under s. 32 of PACE as the arrested person was in the house immediately before being arrested.

C   A search cannot take place in this situation.

D   A search can be carried out under s. 19 of PACE as the constable was lawfully on the premises during the foot chase.

107. BOSS is a predatory sex offender and is in the habit of carrying round a set of handcuffs in his coat should the opportunity arise for him to use them to incapacitate a potential victim. BOSS is interested in buying a house and an acre of land the house sits in from PYKE and he arranges to view the house and land with PYKE showing him around the premises. When he arrives at the house he has the handcuffs in his coat, although he has no intention of using them against PYKE. He is met by PYKE and they enter the land surrounding the house. Shortly afterwards they enter the house. While viewing the house BOSS makes a series of derogatory comments about the kitchen leading to an argument between BOSS and PYKE. PYKE tells BOSS to leave the premises and that he is now a trespasser. BOSS produces the handcuffs and tells PYKE, '*I should hit you with these!*' before storming out of the house and leaving the premises.

At what point, if at all, does BOSS first commit the offence of trespass with a weapon of offence (contrary to s. 8(1) of the Criminal Law Act 1977)?

A   When he first enters the land surrounding the house.

B   When he enters the house.

C   When he is told to leave and produces the handcuffs.

D   The offence is not committed.

108. DC HADDOW wishes to mount a covert surveillance operation on the car park of a leisure centre which is being used to facilitate the sale of drugs. The officer wishes to use several observation points situated around the car park and from these points he wishes to film the activities of persons driving onto the car park as they buy and sell drugs. DC HADDOW completes an application for directed surveillance on the car park.

Which of the following comments is correct with regard to the authorisation of such surveillance?

A A superintendent will authorise this activity; unless it is renewed the authorisation will cease to have effect after three months beginning on the day it was granted.

B A superintendent will authorise this activity; unless it is renewed the authorisation will cease to have effect after one month beginning on the day it was granted.

C An inspector will authorise this activity; unless it is renewed the authorisation will cease to have effect after three months beginning on the day it was granted.

D An inspector will authorise this activity; unless it is renewed that authorisation will cease to have effect after one month beginning on the day it was granted.

109. RYAN has an argument with his neighbour, GIBSON, over parking outside their respective houses. RYAN decides to sabotage GIBSON's car satellite navigation system to get revenge over the parking issue but has no idea how to get into GIBSON's car or how to disable the car alarm. He contacts MOBSBY (who works in a garage) and asks him to disable GIBSON's alarm system and open the car door so that he can damage the satellite navigation system. MOBSBY agrees and in the early hours of the morning he opens the bonnet of GIBSON's car and cuts a wire to the alarm. This does not work and the alarm goes off and MOBSBY escapes.

Considering the offence of interfering with vehicles (contrary to s. 9 of the Criminal Attempts Act 1981) only, which of the statements below is correct?

A Because the interference was carried out in order for RYAN to commit an offence rather than MOBSBY, the offence of interfering with vehicles is not committed.

B No offence is committed because the interference was carried out in order for an offence of criminal damage to be committed.

C MOBSBY must intend to commit an offence of taking and driving away without consent (s. 12(1) of the Theft Act 1968), otherwise the offence cannot be committed.

D No offence is committed as MOBSBY did not interfere with anything carried in or on the motor vehicle.

110. THOMAS is having problems with his neighbour, ABILANT. The two have had a number of arguments during which THOMAS has been humiliated by ABILANT in the street outside their houses. THOMAS is extremely angry about this and wants to get his revenge on ABILANT. He approaches a criminal contact, HOWARD, and asks HOWARD to provide him with a firearm. He tells HOWARD he wants the firearm to '*make ABILANT think he's going to get shot*'. HOWARD does not trust THOMAS with a real firearm so gives him an imitation revolver but tells THOMAS that it is real and loaded. Believing that he has a real firearm THOMAS returns to his house and sees ABILANT cleaning his car in the street. THOMAS approaches ABILANT and putting the revolver to ABILANT's head he states, '*the next time you and I argue will be the last time you live—do you understand?*'

Who, if anyone, commits the offence under s. 16A of the Firearms Act 1968?

A The offence is not committed as an imitation firearm and not a real firearm was used.
B Both THOMAS and HOWARD commit the offence.
C Only THOMAS will commit the offence in these circumstances.
D Only HOWARD will commit the offence in these circumstances.

111. The Magistrates' Courts Act 1980 contains provisions in respect of the mode of trial for juveniles who have committed offences.

Which of the following statements is correct regarding those provisions?

A A juvenile found guilty of an indictable offence in the youth court must be sentenced in an adult court.
B If a juvenile is charged with an indictable offence then he/she must be tried in the Crown Court for the offence.
C A juvenile could never be tried in an adult magistrates' court.
D The general principle is that persons under the age of 18 years should be tried and sentenced in the youth court for both summary and indictable offences.

112. At 5.30 pm, a car driven carelessly by TRICKETT is involved in an accident during which YORK (a pedestrian) is seriously injured. TRICKETT does not stop at the scene of the accident. YORK is taken to hospital but at 10.00 pm the same evening he dies from injuries sustained in the accident. The police are making enquiries to locate TRICKETT and require a specimen from him under s. 7 of the Road Traffic Act 1988.

What is the latest time that TRICKETT can be asked to provide the specimen where a refusal would constitute an offence under s. 3A of the Act (causing death by careless driving when unfit through drink or drugs)?

A Within 18 hours of 5.30 pm (the time of the accident).
B Within 18 hours of 10.00 pm (the time of death).
C Within 24 hours of 5.30 pm (the time of the accident).
D Within 24 hours of 10.00 pm (the time of death).

113. Inspector POVEY is in charge of a highly specialised surveillance unit staffed entirely by male officers. A vacancy occurs within the unit and Inspector POVEY, who is keen to recruit a female officer, drafts an advertisement for the post. In an attempt to recruit a female police officer, the advertisement excludes male applicants.

Which of the following statements is correct with regard to the advertisement?

A The advertisement would be permitted as this is classed as 'positive action'.
B The advertisement would be allowed as Inspector POVEY can 'justify' the reason for excluding male officers.
C If the advertisement was allowed then any male officer could complain about it on the grounds of 'victimisation'.
D The advertisement would be unlawful as it would be classed as 'positive discrimination'.

114. REDMAN is short of money and decides to steal some property to sell to a handler REDMAN is acquainted with. He visits a campsite and enters a tent belonging to INCE and once inside the tent he steals £50 cash hidden inside some cooking equipment. He leaves the tent and then enters an unfinished building on the campsite where he steals several power tools. He then enters a large portable container that has been on the site for three years and is used to store camping equipment. The container has an electricity supply and doors.

At what point, if at all, does REDMAN first commit an offence of burglary?

A When he enters the tent owned by INCE.
B When he enters the unfinished building.
C When he enters the portable container.
D An offence of burglary is not made out in this situation.

115. HEASON lives in a quiet cul-de-sac and is the owner of an old Vauxhall Nova motor vehicle which he keeps parked outside his house; a significant part of the vehicle is parked on the pavement. The vehicle has no wheels and has had the engine and other major parts removed so that all that is left of it is the chassis of the vehicle. The vehicle is not actually causing an obstruction but has the potential to do so in the future. PC LAWTON, on uniform foot patrol, visits the cul-de-sac and sees HEASON's vehicle.

Considering the police power to remove vehicles from the road (under reg. 3 of the Removal and Disposal of Vehicles Regulations 1986) only, does PC LAWTON have to require HEASON to move the vehicle?

A No, as this power can only be used to require the driver of a vehicle, and not the owner, to move it.
B Yes, as the vehicle has the potential to obstruct other road users at some time in the future.
C No, because the chassis is not actually obstructing traffic or other road users.
D Yes, but only because PC LAWTON is in uniform.

116. Orchards Glass Co. Ltd. (a large UPVC manufacturing corporation) is being taken to court for a number of traffic-related offences and it is necessary to serve a summons on the company. The summons is sent by first-class post to the principal office of Orchards Glass Co. Ltd.

Which of the statements below is correct?

A The summons has been served incorrectly as it needs to be physically handed to a person holding a senior position in the corporation.

B A summons can be served on a corporation by post but this must be by recorded delivery.

C This method of service complies with the Criminal Procedure Rules of 2005.

D A summons served on a corporation must be served by handing it to that corporation's legal representative.

117. DC ELLIS takes part in an operation targeting ISGROVE who is a known drugs dealer. A warrant under s. 23 of the Misuse of Drugs Act 1971 is executed at ISGROVE's house at 5.00 am one morning and ISGROVE is arrested for drugs offences. A search of ISGROVE's house is made whilst he is present and during the search a quantity of heroin is found along with a large quantity of money. DC ELLIS asks ISGROVE who the heroin belongs to and where the large quantity of money has come from. ISGROVE is brought to the police station and has a consultation with his solicitor, LEWIS. LEWIS complains to PS MATHERS (the custody officer) that his client has been interviewed during the course of the search at his house.

Considering interviews (for the purpose of Code C of the Codes of Practice), which of the comments below is true?

A DC ELLIS should not have asked any questions of ISGROVE because he is under arrest and therefore can only be asked questions at a police station.

B As long as ISGROVE has been cautioned, there is no restriction on how many questions DC ELLIS may ask of him in relation to the recovered property.

C DC ELLIS's questions have not gone beyond those needed for the immediate investigation of the offence.

D The questions that DC ELLIS has put to ISGROVE are unnecessary for the immediate investigation of the offence and breach the Codes of Practice.

118. Youth Justice Boards provide the framework, context and information base from within which local authorities and youth offending teams operate. The board members are appointed by the Secretary of State.

How many members does such a board consist of?

A Up to 6 members.

B Up to 8 members.

C Up to 10 members.

D Up to 12 members.

119. GREELEY is a keen fan of the pop group U2 and learns that they are to perform a special charity concert in support of the Amnesty International organisation. Entry to the concert is free of charge but by personal invitation only and GREELEY does not have an invitation. Undeterred, GREELEY goes to the concert venue and, managing to avoid the security staff, he sneaks into the concert arena. The concert begins and GREELEY is able to watch the group perform for an hour before being discovered and ejected from the venue.

Which of the statements below is correct with regard to GREELEY's liability for an offence of obtaining a service dishonestly (contrary to s. 11 of the Fraud Act 2006)?

   A The fact that the concert has been put on for free makes no difference, GREELEY has obtained a 'service' and has committed the offence.
   B GREELEY has not committed the offence because he did not use a fraudulent representation or deception to get into the concert arena.
   C GREELEY commits the offence in these circumstances and could be sentenced to six months' imprisonment on summary conviction.
   D GREELEY has not committed the offence in these circumstances as the 'services' of the concert are provided for free.

120. As it is expedient to do so and in order to prevent acts of terrorism (under s. 48 of the Terrorism Act 2000), prohibitions and restrictions on parking are placed in Kestrel Way, a street where ANSIL lives. Appropriate traffic signs are not placed in the street as they were unavailable at the time the order was made. ANSIL is disabled and is in possession of a current disabled person's badge for his vehicle. ANSIL drives into Kestrel Way and parks his vehicle, clearly displaying the disabled person's badge, directly outside his house and goes inside. Moments later, DC TAPLOW (an officer in plain clothes), knocks on ANSIL's door and speaks with ANSIL. DC TAPLOW orders ANSIL to remove his vehicle but ANSIL shuts the door to his house in the officer's face and ignores the officer's request.

Considering the offences and powers under the Terrorism Act 2000, which of the following comments is correct?

   A ANSIL has not committed the offence in this situation.
   B ANSIL commits an offence when he parks his car outside his house in Kestrel Way.
   C ANSIL commits an offence when he parks his car outside his house in Kestrel Way but would have a reasonable excuse to do so as he is in possession of a current disabled person's badge.
   D ANSIL commits an offence when he does not comply with the request from DC TAPLOW to move his vehicle.

121. PC DEVON takes part in an operation to clamp down on vehicles that are being driven in a dangerous condition. A site to stop large numbers of vehicles is identified and the operation goes ahead. PC DEVON stops a significant number of vehicles during the operation and as he does so, considers whether the vehicles require a test certificate under s. 47 of the Road Traffic Act 1988.

In respect of those considerations, which of the statements below is correct?

A A motor vehicle having more than six seats (excluding the driver's seat) which is used to carry passengers would need to be tested one year after its first registration.

B A motor vehicle manufactured abroad would need to be tested two years after its first registration.

C All ambulances are exempt from the requirements to have a test certificate.

D A taxi would need to be tested one year after its first registration.

122. HUTTON and FELIX are both sex offenders who are subject to the requirements of s. 82 of the Sexual Offences Act 2003 (notification periods). HUTTON was sentenced to a period of four years' imprisonment for an offence of assault by penetration (contrary to s. 2 of the Sexual Offences Act 2003) and FELIX was sentenced to a period of eight months' imprisonment for an offence of sexual touching (contrary to s. 3 of the Sexual Offences Act 2003).

How long will HUTTON and FELIX be subject to the notification periods?

A HUTTON for an indefinite period; FELIX for 10 years.

B HUTTON for an indefinite period; FELIX for 7 years.

C HUTTON for 10 years; FELIX for 5 years.

D Hutton for 10 years; FELIX for 2 years.

123. NEWMAN (a resident of the United Kingdom) goes on a business trip to Turkey. During his trip he is in a restaurant when he overhears a conversation between two men who are talking about planting a bomb at Heathrow Airport in a month's time. The men state that the bomb should kill hundreds of people and that when it explodes they will claim it as a victory for al-Qaeda against the British government. NEWMAN flies home to England two days later.

With regard to the offence of information about acts of terrorism (contrary to s. 38B of the Terrorism Act 2000), which of the comments below is correct?

A NEWMAN must disclose the information and this disclosure can be made to any person in authority.

B Should NEWMAN fail to disclose the information he commits an offence punishable by five years' imprisonment.

C As NEWMAN was outside the country when he became aware of the information he could not be charged with the offence if he failed to disclose it.

D There is no defence to this offence.

124. HULLEN works in a postal office for the Royal Mail. He is separated from his wife and the couple are going through a particularly nasty divorce because HULLEN believes that his wife has had and continues to have an affair. HULLEN wishes to obtain evidence to assist his claims in civil court and believing that his wife is receiving letters from her lover through the post he intercepts, opens and read her mail in the sorting office where he works.

Has HULLEN committed an offence contrary to s. 1(1) of the Regulation of Investigatory Powers Act 2000 (interception of public communications)?

   A No, as this legislation only applies to the interception of communications via a public telecommunication system and not a postal system.
   B Yes, and if found guilty of the offence HULLEN could face a maximum sentence of five years' imprisonment.
   C No, because the interception was not accomplished by the use of an electronic device.
   D Yes, but the offence cannot be prosecuted without the consent of the Director of Public Prosecutions.

125. Section 143 of the Road Traffic Act 1988 states that a person must not use a vehicle on a road without a policy of insurance being in force in relation to the use of the vehicle by that person.

Which of the following statements is correct with regard to s. 143 of the Act?

   A In order to convict a person of an offence you must prove intent or guilty knowledge.
   B If a person allows another to use their vehicle on the express condition that the other person insures it first, the lender cannot be convicted of 'permitting'.
   C Generally, an insurance policy obtained by false representations will not be valid for the purposes of s. 143.
   D There is no defence to an offence under s. 143 as the offence is one of absolute liability.

126. O'SHEA won a Victoria Cross medal during the Second World War and keeps it on display in his house. O'SHEA is the victim of a burglary during which the Victoria Cross medal is stolen. O'SHEA is very upset at the loss and is desperate to have his medal returned to him. He writes out an advertisement offering a £500 reward for the return of the medal and states that there will be no questions asked from the person who returns it. He takes the advertisement to SINGH, a printer, who prints several dozen copies of the advertisement for free. O'SHEA places copies of the printed advertisement on lampposts in his area but takes one to WALLIS, a newsagent, who places the advertisement in his shop window for £1.00 per week.

Who has committed the offence of advertising a reward (contrary to s. 23 of the Theft Act 1968)?

   A O'SHEA only.
   B O'SHEA, SINGH and WALLIS.
   C SINGH and WALLIS only.
   D O'SHEA and WALLIS only.

127. ZAHID is the driver of a Land Rover Discovery motor vehicle. VENESS is sitting in the front passenger seat of the vehicle. ZAHID drives the vehicle into a multi-storey car park but misjudges the height of his vehicle and crashes into the roof of the car park causing serious damage to the roof of his vehicle but no damage to the roof of the car park. ZAHID is not injured but VENESS suffers shock as a consequence of the incident.

Which of the below comments is correct with regard to s. 170 of the Road Traffic Act 1988 (reportable accidents)?

A   This is not a reportable accident as it occurred in a car park and not on a road.
B   This is a reportable accident. ZAHID could report the accident by attending a police station in person and has up to 24 hours to do so.
C   This is not a reportable accident as damage only occurred to ZAHID's vehicle and shock does not qualify as an injury under s. 170 of the Act.
D   This is a reportable accident because of the injury to VENESS (shock).

128. JENSON has strong beliefs in respect of parents' rights to control the behaviour of their children and as such believes that it is perfectly acceptable to chastise his children by hitting them if they do something wrong. JENSON's 9-year-old son disobeys JENSON and as a result, JENSON smacks the back of his son's legs twice. The force of the smacks leaves some mild bruising on the back of his son's legs which is seen by a teacher at the son's school. The matter is reported to the police and PC APPLEY investigates the matter.

Considering the law regarding assaults and the issues around lawful chastisement, which of the following comments is correct?

A   This is an offence of actual bodily harm (contrary to s. 47 of the Offences Against the Person Act 1861) and the lawful chastisement defence cannot be used in answer to such a charge.
B   JENSON has committed an offence of battery (contrary to s. 39 of the Criminal Justice Act 1988) but the defence of lawful chastisement may be available to him.
C   This is an offence of actual bodily harm (contrary to s. 47 of the Offences Against the Person Act 1861) but the defence of lawful chastisement may be available to JENSON.
D   JENSON has committed an offence of battery (contrary to s. 39 of the Criminal Justice Act 1988) and the defence of lawful chastisement cannot be used as ther victim was under 10 years of age.

129. BARLOW and PATEN have been arrested by DC FAIRWEATHER in respect of a s. 20 wounding (contrary to the Offences Against the Persons Act 1861). Both men deny the offence and as a consequence DC FAIRWEATHER has arranged for a video identification parade to take place. BARLOW and PATEN are both of a roughly similar appearance.

In relation to video identification and Code D of the Codes of Practice, which of the following comments is correct?

A BARLOW and PATEN cannot appear on the same set of images as each other.

B BARLOW and PATEN can appear on the same set of images; this must be with at least eight other people.

C BARLOW and PATEN can appear on the same set of images; this must be with at least 10 other people.

D BARLOW and PATEN can appear on the same set of images; this must be with at least 12 other people.

130. At 8 pm in the evening, PC FORREST is on uniform foot patrol and is sent to a report of several youths sniffing glue in a park area. When PC FORREST arrives at the scene he finds Andrew HUDSON (aged 13 years) and his brother Paul HUDSON (aged 15 years) in the park area. The boys are known to PC FORREST who is aware of where they live. Although there is no person sniffing glue, there are several bags containing glue near to both youths who tell the officer that there was a person sniffing glue in the park and although that person has gone, he has told the brothers he will be back in 30 minutes with more glue and that they should try sniffing it. PC FORREST reasonably believes that the brothers need protecting from the anti-social behaviour of the individual sniffing glue.

Considering the officer's powers under s. 30 of the Anti-social Behaviour Act 2003, which of the statements below is true?

A PC FORREST cannot remove either brother because both Andrew and Paul HUDSON are over 12 years of age.

B PC FORREST can only remove Andrew HUDSON to his place of residence.

C PC FORREST cannot remove either brother because the power is only available between the hours of 9 pm and 6 am.

D PC FORREST can remove both Andrew and Paul HUDSON to their place of residence.

131. HYDE is a 24-year-old man with the mental capacity of a 7-year-old child. He picks up a stone in his back garden and throws it over a fence into his neighbour's back garden, breaking the glass of a greenhouse window. HYDE is spoken to by a police officer and tells the officer he was only 'having a laugh' and did not stop to think of what damage might be caused by the stone.

Considering the concept of 'recklessness' as it stands after the case of *R v G and R* [2003] 3 WLR 1060, which of the statements below is correct?

A HYDE would be liable for the damage and the fact that he has a mental age of 7 years old is immaterial.

B HYDE could be prosecuted for the offence as his state of mind would constitute 'objective' recklessness.

C As HYDE was unaware that the risk existed or would exist, he would not be reckless.

D As HYDE has failed to consider an obvious risk, his actions would be considered reckless.

132. BURTON is walking along a road when he becomes involved in an altercation with RICE. RICE has a flick-knife in his pocket, which he has as a general precaution in case he is attacked, which he pulls out on BURTON and threatens him with. BURTON is a carpet fitter and has a bag of tools with him, which he carries in the course of his trade, which includes a hammer. In reaction to the threat from RICE he pulls out the hammer and hits RICE with it.

Who, if anyone, is guilty of an offence of having an offensive weapon in a public place (contrary to s. 1(1) of the Prevention of Crime Act 1953)?

A Only RICE commits the offence.

B Only BURTON commits the offence.

C Both RICE and BURTON will commit the offence.

D This offence is not committed by either RICE or BURTON.

133. ANJOU is short of money and compels his boyfriend, HALE, to stand outside a well-known gay bar and offer sexual services to anyone who walks out of the bar. ANJOU accompanies HALE and tells him he will stand nearby to negotiate a price if anyone expresses interest in HALE's offer. DRAKE walks out of the bar and as he passes HALE, HALE asks him if he wants sexual intercourse with him. When DRAKE tells him he is interested and asks '*How much?*' HALE points at ANJOU (standing nearby) and tells DRAKE he will have to pay ANJOU £100 for the sexual service.

Would HALE be considered a prostitute under the Sexual Offences Act 2003?

A No, only women can be prostitutes.

B Yes, it does not matter that HALE was compelled to act as he did.

C No, because any payment will go to a third party (ANJOU).

D Yes, but only if he actually has sexual intercourse with DRAKE.

134. A large amount of case law has built up around ss. 15(5) and 15(5A) of the Road Traffic Offenders Act 1988. These sections deal with issues of admissibility surrounding the provision of samples of either blood or urine to the defendant when the defendant has provided a sample of blood or urine for analysis in relation to driving offences connected to drink or drugs.

Which of the statements below is correct in relation to that case law?

A The specimen taken from the defendant must be divided at the time and in the presence of the defendant.

B The defendant must be provided with his/her part of the specimen at the time of the division of the specimen.

C There is a free-standing right under common law for the defendant to be informed of his/her entitlement to a part of the sample.

D The requirements of s. 15(5) do not extend to an offence of causing death by dangerous driving (contrary to s. 1 of the Road Traffic Act 1988).

135. DC TOPLEY receives a phone call from MARSHALL who is a bank account manager. MARSHALL states she has opened an account for a customer calling himself 'MARTIN LONG'. 'LONG' provided identification and placed a cheque for £5,000 into his new account. MARSHALL says she recognised 'LONG' as MARTIN LONG (she used to go to school with him). 'LONG' told MARSHALL he would be placing several cheques into the account in the future. DC TOPLEY asks MARSHALL to obtain as much private information as possible from 'LONG' the next time he returns to the bank so that he can further investigate his activities and obtain intelligence.

Considering the law relating to covert human intelligence sources (CHIS), which of the below is correct?

A MARSHALL would not be classed as a CHIS as DC TOPLEY is only attempting to obtain intelligence on his activities.

B The obtaining of further information from 'LONG' would not be classed as 'covert'.

C MARSHALL would not be a CHIS as she has come across the information in the ordinary course of her job.

D DC TOPLEY is asking MARSHALL to do something to further develop or enhance the information and this direction could make her a CHIS.

136. HILL is organising a public procession to demonstrate about the large number of immigrants in his area. The chief constable of the area applies to the district council for the procession to be prohibited and is successful. HILL claims that his rights under Article 10 (freedom of expression) and Article 11 (freedom of assembly and association) of the European Convention on Human Rights have been infringed.

Under s. 7 of the Human Rights Act 1998, within what time limit, if any at all, will HILL have to bring proceedings against the public authority?

A Proceedings must be brought within one year from the date on which the act complained of took place.

B Proceedings must be brought within two years from the date on which the act complained of took place.

C Proceedings must be brought within three years from the date on which the act complained of took place.

D There are no time limits placed on victims and proceedings can be brought at any time.

137. HADDON was warned in relation to an incident of theft and had a complete set of her fingerprints taken while she was in custody. It transpires that some of the fingerprints taken from HADDON are not of sufficient quality to allow satisfactory analysis.

Can HADDON be required to attend a police station and have her fingerprints taken?

A Yes, and once the requirement is made HADDON must be given a period of at least 14 days in which to attend.

B No, this power can only be used if the fingerprints taken from HADDON on the previous occasion do not constitute a complete set of her fingerprints.

C Yes, but only if the requirement is made of HADDON within 1 month of her warning.

D No, because HADDON was warned rather than convicted of a recordable offence.

138. Failing to provide an evidential specimen under s. 7(6) of the Road Traffic Act 1988 will only be proved if the person failing to provide a specimen does so 'without reasonable excuse'.

In which of the scenarios below would the defendant have such a 'reasonable excuse'?

A CARROLAN fails to provide a specimen because of mental anguish caused by the custody officer's behaviour.

B BAYLISS fails to provide a specimen in the belief that the officer making the requirement did not have the authority to do so.

C GADD (a juvenile) fails to provide a specimen because of the absence of an appropriate adult.

D KITSON fails to provide a specimen because he does not understand English.

139. HAMILTON goes on a week's holiday and returns to find that BEAMAN has moved into her house and is denying her access. HAMILTON shouts through the letterbox of the front door that she will get BEAMAN out by getting her friend, WITHERS, to throw him out and beat him up. BEAMAN is frightened and leaves the house via the back door. In the meantime, WITHERS arrives. HAMILTON asks him to act on her behalf and get BEAMAN out of her house. WITHERS goes to the front door of the house and shouts that he will kick the front door off its hinges if BEAMAN does not leave.

Who, if anyone, commits an offence of using or threatening violence to secure entry (contrary to s. 6 (1) of the Criminal Law Act 1977)?

A HAMILTON alone.
B WITHERS alone.
C HAMILTON and WITHERS.
D Neither HAMILTON nor WITHERS commit an offence.

140. The Prosecution of Offences (Custody Time Limits) (Amendment) Regulations 1999 provides for a maximum magistrates' court custody time limit (from first appearance to start of trial) in relation to those charged with summary offences.

What is that time limit?

A 49 days.
B 56 days.
C 63 days.
D 70 days.

141. ANDERSON is a member of a gang involved in a string of high-value mortgage frauds. DC HOBDAY receives information that he will be staying in a suite at a local hotel and will be meeting his criminal associates in the suite during his stay. The officer wishes to place a camera in a house opposite the hotel to photograph and identify members of the gang. The camera DC HOBDAY proposes to use will consistently provide images of the same quality and detail as if the camera was actually present in the hotel suite.

What type of surveillance will this activity constitute?

A This would be directed surveillance as, although the camera will photograph activity in residential premises, it is not present in the hotel suite itself.
B This would be intrusive surveillance due to the quality of the images and the fact that hotel rooms are classed as residential premises.
C This would be both directed and intrusive surveillance as it is for the purpose of a specific investigation and hotel rooms are classed as residential premises.
D This would be directed surveillance as hotel rooms are not classed as residential premises.

142. MUNDY is arrested by PC HUNT for an offence of possession of a controlled drug after the officer exercised her powers under the Misuse of Drugs Act 1971 and found some cannabis in MUNDY's pocket. MUNDY is taken to a police station and is interviewed. MUNDY tells PC HUNT that he found the cannabis in the street several minutes before she arrested him. PC HUNT does not believe MUNDY and thinks he is lying. PC HUNT approaches her supervisor and asks for some advice as to whether a 'special warning' under s. 36 of the Criminal Justice and Public Order Act 1994 would be appropriate.

Which of the responses below would be correct?

A A 'special warning' under s. 36 would not be appropriate because MUNDY has provided an account regarding the presence of the drug.

B A 'special warning' under s. 36 would be appropriate because MUNDY has not answered the officer's questions to her satisfaction.

C A 'special warning' under s. 36 would not be appropriate because MUNDY was arrested for an offence under the Misuse of Drugs Act 1971 and not an offence involving dishonesty.

D A 'special warning' under s. 36 would be appropriate but only if MUNDY has a solicitor present during the course of the interview.

143. FINCH approaches CAVELL (who does not know FINCH) and tells him that unless he kills RUFF immediately, his wife and child will be killed. FINCH produces a gun and several photographs of CAVELL's family and tells him that he has been observed for some time. FINCH gives CAVELL a gun and RUFF's details and believing that FINCH will kill his wife and child, CAVELL goes to RUFF's house and kills him. CAVELL is arrested at the scene and states that the only reason he committed the offence was because he was placed under duress.

Would CAVELL be able to use this defence?

A No, as the threat of harm must be made solely to the person who goes on to commit the relevant offence.

B Yes, as the threat drove CAVELL to commit the offence.

C No, as the defence is not available in respect of an offence of murder.

D Yes, as the offence was carried out immediately after the threat was made.

144. Child safety orders are concerned with a child's potential offending behaviour and were introduced to help prevent children from turning to crime.

Which of the below comments is correct in respect of such child safety orders?

A They relate to children under the age of 12.

B There is no right of appeal in respect of the making of a child safety order.

C Jurisdiction for making such orders rests with the magistrates' family proceedings court.

D The minimum age of a child that an order can be made against is 7.

145. RUPPERT (aged 13 years) and BARN (aged 20 years) are assaulted by FLEET. Evidence from the two victims has been obtained by written statement. FLEET is arrested and charged with s. 47 assaults (contrary to the Offences Against the Person Act 1861) against both victims. FLEET pleads 'not guilty' to the charges and the case is due to be heard in a magistrates' court in four weeks' time. RUPPERT and BARN contact the officer in the case, PC MOSS, and inform the officer that they are very distressed about giving evidence. PC MOSS is considering the potential for special measures to be used to assist the witnesses to give evidence (under s. 24 of the Youth Justice and Criminal Evidence Act 1999).

Could the evidence of RUPPERT and BARN be given to the magistrates' court via a live television link?

A Yes, both RUPPERT and BARN could provide their evidence via a live television link to the magistrates' court.

B No, the provision of evidence via a live television link is only available when the case is being tried in a Crown Court.

C Yes, but only by RUPPERT in this case.

D No, as live link television evidence is only an option to a witness who suffers from a mental or physical disorder.

146. STIRK commits an offence of taking a conveyance without consent (contrary to s. 12(1) of the Theft Act 1968) in respect of an Audi TT. STIRK is driving the vehicle in a sensible manner, obeying speed limits etc. when CHEN, a pensioner, steps out in front of the Audi TT. STIRK cannot avoid hitting CHEN with the vehicle and a collision occurs during which CHEN is seriously injured. STIRK drives away from the scene of the incident and abandons the Audi TT several miles away. STIRK is 5 miles away from the Audi TT when a gang of youths throw stones at the vehicle causing damage to the front windscreen.

Has STIRK committed the offence of aggravated vehicle taking (contrary to s. 12A of the Theft Act 1968)?

A Yes, STIRK has committed the offence and should CHEN die, he could be punished with 14 years' imprisonment.

B No, STIRK has not committed the offence in these circumstances because at no stage was the Audi TT driven in a dangerous manner.

C Yes, STIRK has committed the offence but would have a defence to a charge of aggravated vehicle taking as he can show that he was not in the immediate vicinity of the vehicle when it was damaged by the gang of youths.

D No, STIRK has not committed the offence because the accident in which CHEN was injured was not STIRK's fault.

147. MATRON is the driver of a motor bicycle being driven along a road. The motor bicycle has a sidecar attached to it and TOLLY is sitting in the sidecar as a passenger. MATRON is wearing a helmet that conforms to British Standards but the strap that fastens the helmet is improperly fastened under MATRON's chin. TOLLY is not wearing a helmet at all.

Who, if anyone at all, has committed an offence contrary to s. 16(4) of the Road Traffic Act 1988 (driving or riding on motor cycles in contravention of Regulations)?

A Both MATRON and TOLLY have committed an offence.
B Only TOLLY has committed an offence.
C Only MATRON has committed an offence under the Regulations.
D No offence under the Regulations has been committed.

148. SMITH, MACE and CARTER are all outside a pub and are arguing with BATES. SMITH and MACE threaten BATES and tell him they are going to beat him up. BATES is frightened and runs into a nearby private house, followed by all three men. Once inside the house, CARTER assaults BATES.

Who, if anyone, is guilty of the offence of violent disorder contrary to s. 2 of the Public Order Act 1986?

A CARTER only.
B SMITH and MACE only.
C SMITH, MACE and CARTER.
D The offence of violent disorder has not been made out in this situation.

149. SWAIN has been arrested for an offence of possession of a controlled drug (contrary to s. 5(2) of the Misuse of Drugs Act 1971) and has been brought to a designated police station. After SWAIN's details have been obtained and he has been searched, he is led to a cell by PC FRENCH. On the way to the cell, SWAIN states, '*Your pathetic searches never find anything do they?*' This causes PC FRENCH to believe that SWAIN has more drugs in his possession and he takes SWAIN back to the custody officer.

Which of the statements below is correct in respect of a strip-search of SWAIN?

A A strip-search could be authorised in these circumstances but it will need to be authorised by an officer of the rank of inspector or above.
B If SWAIN is strip-searched and that search involves the exposure of intimate body parts, then at least two persons (other than SWAIN) must be present.
C SWAIN cannot be strip-searched unless the custody officer considers that he is in possession of an article that might bring about harm to another person.
D If PC FRENCH were to remove SWAIN's shoes and socks, this would be considered a strip-search.

150. NUGENT is convicted of an offence of sexual touching and sentenced to three years' imprisonment. He serves two years of his sentence before being released from custody.

Considering the Code of Practice under the Criminal Procedure and Investigations Act 1996, how long should material relating to NUGENT's case be retained?

A Material should be retained until six months from the date of NUGENT's conviction.

B Material should be retained until NUGENT is released from custody.

C Material should be retained until 12 months from the date of NUGENT's conviction.

D Material should be retained until the end of the period that NUGENT was sentenced to imprisonment (three years).

Answer sheet

OXFORD
UNIVERSITY PRESS

Blackstone's Police Sergeants' and Inspectors' Mock Examination Paper 2010

#					#					#				
1	⊏A⊐	⊏B⊐	⊏C⊐	⊏D⊐	51	⊏A⊐	⊏B⊐	⊏C⊐	⊏D⊐	101	⊏A⊐	⊏B⊐	⊏C⊐	⊏D⊐
2	⊏A⊐	⊏B⊐	⊏C⊐	⊏D⊐	52	⊏A⊐	⊏B⊐	⊏C⊐	⊏D⊐	102	⊏A⊐	⊏B⊐	⊏C⊐	⊏D⊐
3	⊏A⊐	⊏B⊐	⊏C⊐	⊏D⊐	53	⊏A⊐	⊏B⊐	⊏C⊐	⊏D⊐	103	⊏A⊐	⊏B⊐	⊏C⊐	⊏D⊐
4	⊏A⊐	⊏B⊐	⊏C⊐	⊏D⊐	54	⊏A⊐	⊏B⊐	⊏C⊐	⊏D⊐	104	⊏A⊐	⊏B⊐	⊏C⊐	⊏D⊐
5	⊏A⊐	⊏B⊐	⊏C⊐	⊏D⊐	55	⊏A⊐	⊏B⊐	⊏C⊐	⊏D⊐	105	⊏A⊐	⊏B⊐	⊏C⊐	⊏D⊐
6	⊏A⊐	⊏B⊐	⊏C⊐	⊏D⊐	56	⊏A⊐	⊏B⊐	⊏C⊐	⊏D⊐	106	⊏A⊐	⊏B⊐	⊏C⊐	⊏D⊐
7	⊏A⊐	⊏B⊐	⊏C⊐	⊏D⊐	57	⊏A⊐	⊏B⊐	⊏C⊐	⊏D⊐	107	⊏A⊐	⊏B⊐	⊏C⊐	⊏D⊐
8	⊏A⊐	⊏B⊐	⊏C⊐	⊏D⊐	58	⊏A⊐	⊏B⊐	⊏C⊐	⊏D⊐	108	⊏A⊐	⊏B⊐	⊏C⊐	⊏D⊐
9	⊏A⊐	⊏B⊐	⊏C⊐	⊏D⊐	59	⊏A⊐	⊏B⊐	⊏C⊐	⊏D⊐	109	⊏A⊐	⊏B⊐	⊏C⊐	⊏D⊐
10	⊏A⊐	⊏B⊐	⊏C⊐	⊏D⊐	60	⊏A⊐	⊏B⊐	⊏C⊐	⊏D⊐	110	⊏A⊐	⊏B⊐	⊏C⊐	⊏D⊐
11	⊏A⊐	⊏B⊐	⊏C⊐	⊏D⊐	61	⊏A⊐	⊏B⊐	⊏C⊐	⊏D⊐	111	⊏A⊐	⊏B⊐	⊏C⊐	⊏D⊐
12	⊏A⊐	⊏B⊐	⊏C⊐	⊏D⊐	62	⊏A⊐	⊏B⊐	⊏C⊐	⊏D⊐	112	⊏A⊐	⊏B⊐	⊏C⊐	⊏D⊐
13	⊏A⊐	⊏B⊐	⊏C⊐	⊏D⊐	63	⊏A⊐	⊏B⊐	⊏C⊐	⊏D⊐	113	⊏A⊐	⊏B⊐	⊏C⊐	⊏D⊐
14	⊏A⊐	⊏B⊐	⊏C⊐	⊏D⊐	64	⊏A⊐	⊏B⊐	⊏C⊐	⊏D⊐	114	⊏A⊐	⊏B⊐	⊏C⊐	⊏D⊐
15	⊏A⊐	⊏B⊐	⊏C⊐	⊏D⊐	65	⊏A⊐	⊏B⊐	⊏C⊐	⊏D⊐	115	⊏A⊐	⊏B⊐	⊏C⊐	⊏D⊐
16	⊏A⊐	⊏B⊐	⊏C⊐	⊏D⊐	66	⊏A⊐	⊏B⊐	⊏C⊐	⊏D⊐	116	⊏A⊐	⊏B⊐	⊏C⊐	⊏D⊐
17	⊏A⊐	⊏B⊐	⊏C⊐	⊏D⊐	67	⊏A⊐	⊏B⊐	⊏C⊐	⊏D⊐	117	⊏A⊐	⊏B⊐	⊏C⊐	⊏D⊐
18	⊏A⊐	⊏B⊐	⊏C⊐	⊏D⊐	68	⊏A⊐	⊏B⊐	⊏C⊐	⊏D⊐	118	⊏A⊐	⊏B⊐	⊏C⊐	⊏D⊐
19	⊏A⊐	⊏B⊐	⊏C⊐	⊏D⊐	69	⊏A⊐	⊏B⊐	⊏C⊐	⊏D⊐	119	⊏A⊐	⊏B⊐	⊏C⊐	⊏D⊐
20	⊏A⊐	⊏B⊐	⊏C⊐	⊏D⊐	70	⊏A⊐	⊏B⊐	⊏C⊐	⊏D⊐	120	⊏A⊐	⊏B⊐	⊏C⊐	⊏D⊐
21	⊏A⊐	⊏B⊐	⊏C⊐	⊏D⊐	71	⊏A⊐	⊏B⊐	⊏C⊐	⊏D⊐	121	⊏A⊐	⊏B⊐	⊏C⊐	⊏D⊐
22	⊏A⊐	⊏B⊐	⊏C⊐	⊏D⊐	72	⊏A⊐	⊏B⊐	⊏C⊐	⊏D⊐	122	⊏A⊐	⊏B⊐	⊏C⊐	⊏D⊐
23	⊏A⊐	⊏B⊐	⊏C⊐	⊏D⊐	73	⊏A⊐	⊏B⊐	⊏C⊐	⊏D⊐	123	⊏A⊐	⊏B⊐	⊏C⊐	⊏D⊐
24	⊏A⊐	⊏B⊐	⊏C⊐	⊏D⊐	74	⊏A⊐	⊏B⊐	⊏C⊐	⊏D⊐	124	⊏A⊐	⊏B⊐	⊏C⊐	⊏D⊐
25	⊏A⊐	⊏B⊐	⊏C⊐	⊏D⊐	75	⊏A⊐	⊏B⊐	⊏C⊐	⊏D⊐	125	⊏A⊐	⊏B⊐	⊏C⊐	⊏D⊐
26	⊏A⊐	⊏B⊐	⊏C⊐	⊏D⊐	76	⊏A⊐	⊏B⊐	⊏C⊐	⊏D⊐	126	⊏A⊐	⊏B⊐	⊏C⊐	⊏D⊐
27	⊏A⊐	⊏B⊐	⊏C⊐	⊏D⊐	77	⊏A⊐	⊏B⊐	⊏C⊐	⊏D⊐	127	⊏A⊐	⊏B⊐	⊏C⊐	⊏D⊐
28	⊏A⊐	⊏B⊐	⊏C⊐	⊏D⊐	78	⊏A⊐	⊏B⊐	⊏C⊐	⊏D⊐	128	⊏A⊐	⊏B⊐	⊏C⊐	⊏D⊐
29	⊏A⊐	⊏B⊐	⊏C⊐	⊏D⊐	79	⊏A⊐	⊏B⊐	⊏C⊐	⊏D⊐	129	⊏A⊐	⊏B⊐	⊏C⊐	⊏D⊐
30	⊏A⊐	⊏B⊐	⊏C⊐	⊏D⊐	80	⊏A⊐	⊏B⊐	⊏C⊐	⊏D⊐	130	⊏A⊐	⊏B⊐	⊏C⊐	⊏D⊐
31	⊏A⊐	⊏B⊐	⊏C⊐	⊏D⊐	81	⊏A⊐	⊏B⊐	⊏C⊐	⊏D⊐	131	⊏A⊐	⊏B⊐	⊏C⊐	⊏D⊐
32	⊏A⊐	⊏B⊐	⊏C⊐	⊏D⊐	82	⊏A⊐	⊏B⊐	⊏C⊐	⊏D⊐	132	⊏A⊐	⊏B⊐	⊏C⊐	⊏D⊐
33	⊏A⊐	⊏B⊐	⊏C⊐	⊏D⊐	83	⊏A⊐	⊏B⊐	⊏C⊐	⊏D⊐	133	⊏A⊐	⊏B⊐	⊏C⊐	⊏D⊐
34	⊏A⊐	⊏B⊐	⊏C⊐	⊏D⊐	84	⊏A⊐	⊏B⊐	⊏C⊐	⊏D⊐	134	⊏A⊐	⊏B⊐	⊏C⊐	⊏D⊐
35	⊏A⊐	⊏B⊐	⊏C⊐	⊏D⊐	85	⊏A⊐	⊏B⊐	⊏C⊐	⊏D⊐	135	⊏A⊐	⊏B⊐	⊏C⊐	⊏D⊐
36	⊏A⊐	⊏B⊐	⊏C⊐	⊏D⊐	86	⊏A⊐	⊏B⊐	⊏C⊐	⊏D⊐	136	⊏A⊐	⊏B⊐	⊏C⊐	⊏D⊐
37	⊏A⊐	⊏B⊐	⊏C⊐	⊏D⊐	87	⊏A⊐	⊏B⊐	⊏C⊐	⊏D⊐	137	⊏A⊐	⊏B⊐	⊏C⊐	⊏D⊐
38	⊏A⊐	⊏B⊐	⊏C⊐	⊏D⊐	88	⊏A⊐	⊏B⊐	⊏C⊐	⊏D⊐	138	⊏A⊐	⊏B⊐	⊏C⊐	⊏D⊐
39	⊏A⊐	⊏B⊐	⊏C⊐	⊏D⊐	89	⊏A⊐	⊏B⊐	⊏C⊐	⊏D⊐	139	⊏A⊐	⊏B⊐	⊏C⊐	⊏D⊐
40	⊏A⊐	⊏B⊐	⊏C⊐	⊏D⊐	90	⊏A⊐	⊏B⊐	⊏C⊐	⊏D⊐	140	⊏A⊐	⊏B⊐	⊏C⊐	⊏D⊐
41	⊏A⊐	⊏B⊐	⊏C⊐	⊏D⊐	91	⊏A⊐	⊏B⊐	⊏C⊐	⊏D⊐	141	⊏A⊐	⊏B⊐	⊏C⊐	⊏D⊐
42	⊏A⊐	⊏B⊐	⊏C⊐	⊏D⊐	92	⊏A⊐	⊏B⊐	⊏C⊐	⊏D⊐	142	⊏A⊐	⊏B⊐	⊏C⊐	⊏D⊐
43	⊏A⊐	⊏B⊐	⊏C⊐	⊏D⊐	93	⊏A⊐	⊏B⊐	⊏C⊐	⊏D⊐	143	⊏A⊐	⊏B⊐	⊏C⊐	⊏D⊐
44	⊏A⊐	⊏B⊐	⊏C⊐	⊏D⊐	94	⊏A⊐	⊏B⊐	⊏C⊐	⊏D⊐	144	⊏A⊐	⊏B⊐	⊏C⊐	⊏D⊐
45	⊏A⊐	⊏B⊐	⊏C⊐	⊏D⊐	95	⊏A⊐	⊏B⊐	⊏C⊐	⊏D⊐	145	⊏A⊐	⊏B⊐	⊏C⊐	⊏D⊐
46	⊏A⊐	⊏B⊐	⊏C⊐	⊏D⊐	96	⊏A⊐	⊏B⊐	⊏C⊐	⊏D⊐	146	⊏A⊐	⊏B⊐	⊏C⊐	⊏D⊐
47	⊏A⊐	⊏B⊐	⊏C⊐	⊏D⊐	97	⊏A⊐	⊏B⊐	⊏C⊐	⊏D⊐	147	⊏A⊐	⊏B⊐	⊏C⊐	⊏D⊐
48	⊏A⊐	⊏B⊐	⊏C⊐	⊏D⊐	98	⊏A⊐	⊏B⊐	⊏C⊐	⊏D⊐	148	⊏A⊐	⊏B⊐	⊏C⊐	⊏D⊐
49	⊏A⊐	⊏B⊐	⊏C⊐	⊏D⊐	99	⊏A⊐	⊏B⊐	⊏C⊐	⊏D⊐	149	⊏A⊐	⊏B⊐	⊏C⊐	⊏D⊐
50	⊏A⊐	⊏B⊐	⊏C⊐	⊏D⊐	100	⊏A⊐	⊏B⊐	⊏C⊐	⊏D⊐	150	⊏A⊐	⊏B⊐	⊏C⊐	⊏D⊐

OXFORD
UNIVERSITY PRESS

**Blackstone's Police Sergeants' and
Inspectors' Mock Examination Paper 2010**

Pack 2

Contents

**DO NOT OPEN THIS ANSWER PACK UNTIL YOU
HAVE COMPLETED THE MOCK EXAM**

Marking Instructions

Lay your answer sheet next to the marking matrix as shown below; you may find it useful to fold the answer sheet to do this. Starting with Question 1, compare your marked answer (in the example below this is 'A') with the correct answer given on the marking matrix. If the correct answer matches your marked answer put a '1' inside the white box on the relevant row. If it does not (see Question 2 below) put a '0'.

Please follow these instructions carefully to ensure accuracy. Marks ('1' or '0') should only be made in the white blank boxes (which indicate the subject area a question is related to)—please do not write anything in the grey boxes.

	Question No.	Correct Answer	Crime	Evidence and Procedure	General Police Duties	Road Policing	Verification Question
1 ▬A▬ ⸤B⸣ ⸤C⸣ ⸤D⸣	1	A	1				
2 ⸤A⸣ ⸤B⸣ ▬C▬ ⸤D⸣	2	B			0		
3 ⸤A⸣ ⸤B⸣ ▬C▬ ⸤D⸣	3	C	1				
4 ⸤A⸣ ▬B▬ ⸤C⸣ ⸤D⸣	4	B				1	
5 ▬A▬ ⸤B⸣ ⸤C⸣ ⸤D⸣	5	A		1			
6 ⸤A⸣ ⸤B⸣ ⸤C⸣ ▬D▬	6	A				0	
7 ⸤A⸣ ▬B▬ ⸤C⸣ ⸤D⸣	7	B					1

When you have marked the first 50 questions, add up the total for each column (Crime, Evidence and Procedure, General Police Duties and Road Policing) and enter the totals into the boxes marked A1, B1, etc. Then transfer these totals into the corresponding box ('A1', 'B1' etc.) on the score sheet.

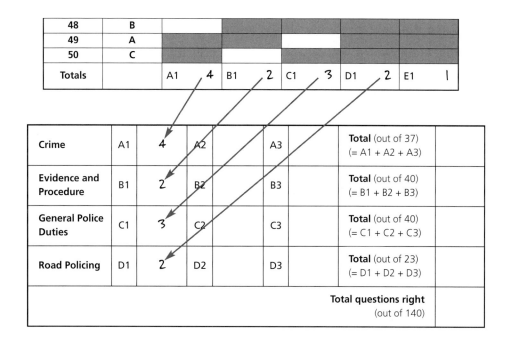

48	B					
49	A					
50	C					
Totals		A1 4	B1 2	C1 3	D1 2	E1 1

							Total	
Crime	A1	4	A2		A3		**Total** (out of 37) (= A1 + A2 + A3)	
Evidence and Procedure	B1	2	B2		B3		**Total** (out of 40) (= B1 + B2 + B3)	
General Police Duties	C1	3	C2		C3		**Total** (out of 40) (= C1 + C2 + C3)	
Road Policing	D1	2	D2		D3		**Total** (out of 23) (= D1 + D2 + D3)	
							Total questions right (out of 140)	

Then do the same for Questions 51 to 100 and fill in boxes A2 to D2 on the score sheet, and finally Questions 101 to 150, which will enable you to fill in boxes A3 to D3 on the score sheet.

Total up A1 + A2 + A3, which will give you a score for Crime. Then do the same for Evidence and Procedure, General Police Duties and Road Policing. You will then have a total for each subject area, which you can add up to reach a final total for the whole exam.

Compare your final total to the table underneath the score sheet, which will indicate whether or not you have passed the mock examination.

The pass mark for the sergeants' examination is 77 (55%).

The pass mark for the inspectors' examination is 91 (65%).

Marking Matrix, Questions 1–50

Question No.	Correct Answer	Crime	Evidence and Procedure	General Police Duties	Road Policing	Verification Question
1	A	X				
2	B			X		
3	C	X				
4	B				X	
5	A		X			
6	A				X	
7	B					X
8	D			X		
9	D		X			
10	C			X		
11	B		X			
12	B	X				
13	A	X				
14	C		X			
15	B			X		
16	D		X			
17	A			X		
18	A		X			
19	C			X		
20	C	X				
21	B		X			
22	C			X		
23	C		X			
24	A			X		
25	D	X				
26	D			X		
27	D				X	
28	C		X			
29	B	X				
30	B			X		
31	A		X			
32	B					X
33	D	X				
34	A			X		
35	D			X		
36	B			X		
37	B		X			
38	C		X			
39	C	X				
40	C			X		
41	A		X			
42	B	X				
43	C				X	
44	B					X
45	D			X		
46	D		X			
47	B		X			
48	B	X				
49	A			X		
50	C		X			
Totals		A1	B1	C1	D1	E1

Marking Matrix, Questions 51–100

Question No.	Correct Answer	Crime	Evidence and Procedure	General Police Duties	Road Policing	Verification Question
51	C	X				
52	A					X
53	A		X			
54	B		X			
55	A	X				
56	C	A2	B2	C2	D2	E2
57	C	X				
58	B			X		
59	D		X			
60	D	X				
61	B		X			
62	C			X		
63	A		X			
64	A				X	
65	B			X		
66	D			X		
67	C				X	
68	A	X				
69	D					X
70	B	X				
71	B				X	
72	C		X			
73	C			X		
74	D	X				
75	D	X				
76	B			X		
77	A	X				
78	C	X				
79	B				X	
80	D				X	
81	D					X
82	A			X		
83	D	X				
84	B		X			
85	C	X				
86	C	X				
87	C			X		
88	A				X	
89	D		X			
90	C				X	
91	A					X
92	B			X		
93	A	X				
94	C				X	
95	D		X			
96	D				X	
97	B			X		
98	B	X				
99	A	X				
100	A	X				
Totals		A2	B2	C2	D2	E2

Marking Matrix, Questions 101–150

Question No.	Correct Answer	Crime	Evidence and Procedure	General Police Duties	Road Policing	Verification Question
101	B		☐			
102	A	☐				
103	D				☐	
104	A			☐		
105	C		☐			
106	C			☐		
107	D			☐		
108	A			☐		
109	B	☐				
110	B			☐		
111	D					☐
112	A				☐	
113	D			☐		
114	B	☐				
115	B				☐	
116	C		☐			
117	C		☐			
118	D		☐			
119	D	☐				
120	A				☐	
121	D				☐	
122	A	☐				
123	B			☐		
124	D			☐		
125	B				☐	
126	B	☐		☐		
127	D				☐	
128	B					☐
129	D		☐			
130	C			☐		
131	C	☐				
132	A			☐		
133	B	☐				
134	D				☐	
135	D			☐		
136	A			☐		
137	C		☐			
138	D				☐	
139	D					☐
140	B			☐		
141	B			☐		
142	A		☐			
143	C	☐				
144	C		☐			
145	C		☐			
146	A	☐				
147	C				☐	
148	C			☐		
149	B		☐			
150	B		☐			
Totals		A3	B3	C3	D3	E3

Score Sheet

(Please note that your score for verification questions is not included on this score sheet.)

Crime	A1		A2		A3		Total (out of 38) (= A1 + A2 + A3)	
Evidence and Procedure	B1		B2		B3		Total (out of 39) (= B1 + B2 + B3)	
General Police Duties	C1		C2		C3		Total (out of 40) (= C1 + C2 + C3)	
Road Policing	D1		D2		D3		Total (out of 23) (= D1 + D2 + D3)	
							Total questions right (out of 140)	

Questions right	% score	Questions right	% score	Questions right	% score	Questions right	% score	Questions right	% score
1	0.714	29	20.714	57	40.714	85	60.714	113	80.714
2	1.428	30	21.428	58	41.428	86	61.428	114	81.428
3	2.142	31	22.142	59	42.142	87	62.142	115	82.142
4	2.857	32	22.857	60	42.857	88	62.857	116	82.857
5	3.571	33	23.571	61	43.571	89	63.571	117	83.571
6	4.285	34	24.285	62	44.285	90	64.285	118	84.285
7	5	35	25	63	45	91	65 (pass)	119	85
8	5.714	36	25.714	64	45.714	92	65.714	120	85.714
9	6.428	37	26.428	65	46.428	93	66.428	121	86.428
10	7.142	38	27.142	66	47.142	94	67.142	122	87.142
11	7.857	39	27.857	67	47.857	95	67.857	123	87.857
12	8.571	40	28.571	68	48.571	96	68.571	124	88.571
13	9.285	41	29.285	69	49.285	97	69.285	125	89.285
14	10	42	30	70	50	98	70	126	90
15	10.714	43	30.714	71	50.714	99	70.714	127	90.714
16	11.428	44	31.428	72	51.428	100	71.428	128	91.428
17	12.142	45	32.142	73	52.142	101	72.142	129	92.142
18	12.857	46	32.857	74	52.857	102	72.857	130	92.857
19	13.571	47	33.571	75	53.571	103	73.571	131	93.571
20	14.285	48	34.285	76	54.285	104	74.285	132	94.285
21	15	49	35	77	55 (pass)	105	75	133	95
22	15.714	50	35.714	78	55.714	106	75.714	134	95.714
23	16.428	51	36.428	79	56.428	107	76.428	135	96.428
24	17.142	52	37.142	80	57.142	108	77.142	136	97.142
25	17.857	53	37.857	81	57.857	109	77.857	137	97.857
26	18.571	54	38.571	82	58.571	110	78.571	138	98.571
27	19.285	55	39.285	83	59.285	111	79.285	139	99.285
28	20	56	40	84	60	112	80	140	100

OXFORD
UNIVERSITY PRESS

**Blackstone's Police Sergeants' and
Inspectors' Mock Examination Paper 2010**

Answer Booklet

1. Answer **A** — For an offence to be committed the general approach is that the *mens rea* (state of mind, i.e. intent or recklessness) will be present in the defendant's mind at the time of the *actus reus* (the criminal conduct, i.e. the physical act). However, the state of mind for an offence may occur after the *actus reus*, so you have a situation where the criminal mind 'catches up' with the criminal body. When ROTHEN drives onto PC SIMPSON's foot he commits the *actus reus* of an assault (in this case a s. 47 assault as CPS charging standards place extensive bruising in that category, therefore answer C is incorrect), but at this stage he has committed no offence as he has only responded to the officer's request. At this stage the injury is accidental. However, when PC SIMPSON requests ROTHEN to move his car and he is told to wait, the *mens rea* for an offence of assault comes into existence. *Mens rea* and *actus reus* have to co-exist at some point in time but they do not have to actually start at the same time (making answer B incorrect). Answer D is incorrect as recklessness is a relevant state of mind for several assault offences (s. 39 of the Criminal Justice Act 1988, ss. 47 and 20 of the Offences Against the Person Act 1861).

    Crime, paras 1.2.2.2, 1.7.2.5, 1.7.3.1, 1.7.6.1

2. Answer **B** — There is no authorisation level required for the powers under s. 50 of the Act to be used, making answer A incorrect. Seize and sift powers can only be used if it can be shown that it was *essential* to do so, rather than simply convenient or preferable to do so, making answer D incorrect. The kind of material that is allowed to be removed from premises includes, for example, material stored on a computer or where it is not reasonably practicable to sort through material at the scene. The powers under s. 50 only extend the scope of some other existing power, i.e. they do not provide freestanding powers to search and seize property, making answer C incorrect.

    General Police Duties, para. 4.4.17.1

3. Answer **C** — Section 8 of the Theft Act 1968 states that a person is guilty of robbery if he steals, and immediately before or at the time of doing so, and in order to do so, he uses force on any person or puts or seeks to put any person in fear of being then and there subjected to force. When force is used, it need not be on the victim of the theft so when JOFEMAR knocks AMES off-balance and steals cash belonging to the supermarket it is still a robbery, making answer A incorrect. The amount of 'force' used in order to accomplish the offence of theft need only be minimal, e.g. a push or shove (*R v Dawson* (1976) 64 Cr App R 170), making answer B incorrect.

The force must be used or threatened 'in order to' commit the theft; force used for any other reason is not robbery. Therefore when force is threatened against the police officer in order to escape, this is not robbery, making answer D incorrect.

Crime, para. 1.12.9

4. Answer **B** — Section 7(2) of the Road Traffic Act 1988 states that a requirement to provide a specimen of breath can be made at a police station, a hospital or at or near a place where a relevant breath test has been administered to the person concerned or would have been so administered but for his failure to co-operate with it, making answer A incorrect. The fact that a person is too drunk to provide a sample may be regarded as a 'medical' reason for requiring a sample of blood/urine (*Young* v *DPP* [1992] RTR 328), making answer C incorrect. For the officer making the requirement to have 'reasonable cause to believe' that medical reasons exist, there is no need to seek medical advice first (*Dempsey* v *Catton* [1986] RTR 194).

Road Policing, paras 3.5.5 to 3.5.5.4

5. Answer **A** — When a person is released on bail under s. 30A(1) and a specific police station has been named for the person bailed to attend and conditions have been attached to that bail, the conditions can be varied. This can be accomplished by the person concerned applying to a magistrates' court to do so or by attending at the specified police station he/she was bailed to and by speaking to a 'relevant officer' (usually the custody officer). This makes answer D incorrect (although the conditions can be varied by a magistrates' court as an alternative to attending the police station specified as above). As bail conditions can be varied by a 'relevant officer', answer B is incorrect. In fact, a constable involved in the investigation should not deal with the request unless no other constable is available (s. 30CA(5)). Answer C is incorrect as when bail has been granted and a specific police station named for the person to attend, the person bailed can only apply for conditions to be varied at that particular police station (or a magistrates' court).

Evidence and Procedure, para. 2.4.2.5

6. Answer **A** — Section 6(5) of the Road Traffic Act 1988 states that if an accident occurs owing to the presence of a motor vehicle on a road or other public place and a constable reasonably believes that the person was driving, attempting to drive, or in charge of the vehicle at the time of the accident they may require a preliminary test to take place. You must show that an accident had taken place, not simply believed that to be the case. Answer B is incorrect as, apart from the fact the requirement cannot be made, the preliminary test may take place at or near the place where the requirement to co-operate with the test is imposed *or* if the constable who imposes the requirement thinks it expedient, at a police station specified by him/her. Answer C is incorrect as if an accident has taken place there is no need for the officer making the requirement to believe or even suspect that the person has been drinking. Answer D is incorrect as there is no need for the officer to believe or suspect that any offence has taken place.

Road Policing, para. 3.5.4.3

7. Answer **B** — The offence under s. 63 of the Act will not cover animated images, such as cartoon characters. This is because one of the requirements of the offence is that a reasonable person looking at the image would think that the people/animals portrayed were real. This means that

answers A and C are incorrect. To qualify as an extreme pornographic image, an image must satisfy several elements:

- that the image is pornographic;
- that the image is grossly offensive, disgusting or otherwise obscene in character; and
- that the image portrays in an explicit and realistic way one of several acts — one of those acts is a person performing an act of intercourse or oral sex with an animal (whether dead or alive) (bestiality).

Section 66 of the Act provides a defence for those who participate in the creation of extreme pornographic images but the defence is limited and does not cover images relating to bestiality, making answer D incorrect.

VERIFICATION QUESTION, Crime, para. 1.9.6

8. Answer **D** — The Race Relations Act 1976 aims to control discrimination on the grounds of colour, race, nationality, ethnic and national origins— it has nothing to do with sexuality or religion, making answer A incorrect. Answer B is incorrect; although ethnic group is a broad definition which may include any group with a shared culture or history, it *does not* include Rastafarians (*Crown Suppliers v Dawkins* [1993] ICR 517). Answer C is incorrect as speakers of a particular language (e.g. Welsh) are *not* an ethnic group *per se* (*Gwynedd County Council v Jones* [1986] ICR 833).

General Police Duties, para. 4.13.3

9. Answer **D** — Section 64A of the Police and Criminal Evidence Act 1984 states that a person may be photographed whilst they are detained at a police station (see also Code 'D' para. 5.12). There is no requirement that they be charged with an offence, making answer A incorrect. Such photographs can be taken by a constable or a designated detention officer, making answer B incorrect. The photograph need not be taken by an individual who is the same sex as the person to be photographed, making answer C incorrect. Reasonable force can be used to obtain the photograph (Code 'D' para. 5.14).

Evidence and Procedure, para. 2.10.12

10. Answer **C** — Under s. 179(1) of the Licensing Act 2003, where a constable or authorised person has reason to believe that any premises are being, or are about to be, used for licensable activities, they may enter the premises with a view to seeing whether the activity is being, or is to be, carried out in accordance with an authorisation.

General Police Duties, para. 4.11.2.3

11. Answer **B** — Prisoners who will be detained (or are likely to be detained) for more than six hours must go to a 'designated' police station.

Evidence and Procedure, para. 2.10.4

12. Answer **B** — The only person who would be covered by the legislation is the member of Her Majesty's Coastguard — none of the other individuals named are protected by the legislation.

Crime, para. 1.7.4.1

13. Answer **A** — The defence under s. 5 of the Misuse of Drugs Act 1971 is available as a defence to the charge of unlawful possession only (s. 5 of the Misuse of Drugs Act 1971), making answer B incorrect. The defence is available to a charge of possession no matter what type/class of drug it is alleged the defendant has possession of, making answer D incorrect. Answer C is incorrect as the defence (under s. 5(4)(a)) is available to a person who, knowing or suspecting the substance to be a controlled drug, took possession of it to prevent another committing or continuing to commit an offence in connection with that drug and that as soon as possible after taking possession of it he took all such steps as were reasonably open to him to destroy the drug or to deliver it into the custody of a person lawfully entitled to take custody of it. RAINWAY commits the offence because she does not deliver it into the possession of such a person as soon as possible after taking possession of it.

Crime, para. 1.6.4.1

14. Answer **C** — If a suspect appears to be deaf or there is any doubt about his/her hearing or speaking ability, an interpreter should be found (unless he/she agrees in writing to proceed without an interpreter) (Code C, para. 13.5). This makes answers A, B and D incorrect.

Evidence and Procedure, para. 2.12.9.15

15. Answer **B** — Muslims, Catholics, atheists, and Rastafarians are all subject to the racially and religiously aggravated offences created by ss. 28 to 32 of the Crime and Disorder Act 1998. Atheists have always been included in the definition as per s. 28(5): 'In this section "religious group" means a group of persons defined by reference to religious belief *or lack of religious belief.*' Since the Anti-terrorism, Crime and Security Act 2001, religious groups from all denominations have been protected by the legislation. The offences of causing grievous bodily harm (contrary to s. 18 of the Offences Against the Person Act 1861), aggravated criminal damage (contrary to s. 1(2) of the Criminal Damage Act 1971) and affray (contrary to s. 3 of the Public Order Act 1986) are not covered by the Crime and Disorder Act 1998 and therefore cannot be racially aggravated.

General Police Duties, paras 4.5.2 to 4.5.2.7

16. Answer **D** — Answer A has not complied with the Codes of Practice as a dental impression (an intimate sample) can only be taken by a registered dentist. Answer B has not complied as a swab taken from the genitals is an intimate sample and such samples cannot be taken by police officers (unless it is urine as per answer D). A sample from under a nail is not an intimate sample; it is a non-intimate sample therefore answer C is incorrect.

Evidence and Procedure, paras 2.11.5.1 to 2.11.6.7

17. Answer **A** — A police friend can be a police officer, a police staff member or a person nominated by the police officer's staff association. Unless the police officer concerned has the right to be legally represented and chooses to be so represented, the police friend can represent the police officer concerned at the misconduct proceedings, performance proceedings, appeal meeting, a special case hearing or at a police appeals tribunal, making answer B incorrect. Answer C is incorrect as if a police officer is interviewed in connection with a criminal matter committed whilst off duty which has no connection with his/her role as a serving police officer, the police friend has *no* right to

attend the criminal interview of that police officer. Answer D is incorrect as a police friend who has agreed to accompany a police officer would be considered 'on duty' when attending interviews, meetings or hearings.

General Police Duties, para. 4.1.10

18. Answer **A** — Section 25 of the Criminal Justice and Public Order Act 1994 applies when a defendant is charged with murder, attempted murder, manslaughter, and a host of offences under the Sexual Offences Act 2003 and has a conviction for one of those offences. This makes answer D incorrect. There are no time limitations relating to when the previous conviction was obtained, making answer B incorrect. A defendant charged with one of the above offences, and with a previous conviction for one of the above offences, will not be granted bail unless there are exceptional circumstances which justify it, making answer C incorrect.

Evidence and Procedure, para. 2.4.5

19. Answer **C** — When exercising discretionary powers to prevent disorder, police officers will be expected to focus their attention on those who are likely to present the actual threat of violence or disorder (as per the decision in *Redmond-Bate* v *DPP* [1999] Crim LR 998). In this case that would be SENNOR and not HERRICK, making answer A incorrect. A breach of the peace can take place in public or in private, making answer B incorrect. Answer D is incorrect as there is no requirement to show that a disturbance in private property affected members of the public outside that property.

General Police Duties, para. 4.6.2 to 4.6.2.1

20. Answer **C** — The offence under s. 1 of the Child Abduction Act 1984 can only be committed if the child in question is taken out of the United Kingdom without the appropriate consent— Scotland is part of the United Kingdom so the offence is not committed.

Crime, para. 1.11.3.1

21. Answer **B** — In the case of *Gizzinio* v *Chief Constable of Derbyshire* [1998] EWCA CIV 534, Gizzinio had been remanded in custody in respect of certain charges that were not ultimately pursued. Damages (for the wrongful exercise of authority) were sought on the basis that the police had wrongly opposed the granting of bail. It was held that the decision regarding bail is part of the process of the investigation of crime with a view to prosecution and so the police enjoyed immunity in that respect, making answer A incorrect. Answer C is incorrect as bail can be granted to an individual immaterial of whether the offence was committed in England or Wales or elsewhere, and immaterial as to which country's law the offence relates (s. 15). Answer D is incorrect as there is no time limit for which bail may be granted under the Police and Criminal Evidence Act 1984.

Evidence and Procedure, paras 2.4.1, 2.4.3, 2.4.5.1, 2.4.6.8

22. Answer **C** — Code A of the Codes of Practice (para. 3.11) states that if a person does not appear to understand what is being said, or there is any doubt about their ability to understand English, the officer must take all reasonable steps to bring the relevant information (constable's name, etc.) to the person's attention, making answer D incorrect. The relevant information must be given *before*

starting the search (making answer B incorrect). The fact that MALIK does not understand the officer does not preclude the use of the powers under s. 1 PACE, making answer A incorrect.

General Police Duties, para. 4.4.4.7

23. Answer **C** — If the custody officer decides to detain CRANE in police detention then the maximum period he may detain him will not exceed six hours beginning when the person was charged with the offence.

Evidence and Procedure, para. 2.10.15

24. Answer **A** — An affray is committed when a person uses or threatens unlawful violence, meaning that no offence is committed when TYRONE stands outside PERCY's house staring into the lounge window. The offence cannot be committed by the use of words alone (s. 3(3)), meaning that no offence is committed when TYRONE shouts at PERCY. However, if there is some action then the offence can be committed (such as using a dog to threaten violence; *R* v *Dixon* [1993] Crim LR 579).

General Police Duties, para. 4.6.6

25. Answer **D** — Fruit growing wild on *any* land is not considered property unless, when it is actually picked, it is done so for reward, sale or other commercial purpose. This purpose must exist at the time of picking. Therefore, JORDAN does not commit the offence of theft as his intention to sell the jam he made from the berries was not in existence at the time the picking took place.

Crime, para. 1.12.2.4

26. Answer **D** — Regulation 6 of the Police (Promotion) Regulations 1996 states that a member of a police force who is required to perform the duties of a higher rank may, *even though there is no vacancy for that rank*, be promoted temporarily to it, but, in the case of promotion to the rank of *sergeant or inspector, only if he is qualified for promotion under regulation 3*. An officer must be qualified to the rank to perform the duties of a sergeant or inspector, making answers A and C incorrect. It is immaterial whether a vacancy exists for an officer of that rank, making answer B incorrect.

General Police Duties, para. 4.4.2.1

27. Answer **D** — The offence of using a motor vehicle without insurance takes place on a road or public place— car parks are public places (*Cutter* v *Eagle Star Insurance Co. Ltd* [1998] 4 All ER 417). The offence is punishable with a fine and/or a discretionary disqualification, making answer B incorrect. There is a defence to the offence (making answer C incorrect) under s. 143(3) which states that a person will not be convicted if:

- the vehicle does not belong to them and it was in their possession under a contract of hiring or loan; and
- that the person was using the vehicle in the course of their employment; and
- that the person neither knew nor had reason to believe that there was not in force in relation to the vehicle such a policy of insurance or security.

As YAU is not employed by RICHARDSON the defence is not available and so answer A is incorrect.

Road Policing, paras 3.6.2 to 3.6.2.2

28. Answer **C** — The prosecutor's opinion is only relevant to primary disclosure. After primary disclosure, disclosure is subject to a wider test in that the test is objective, i.e. it requires disclosure where any reasonable person would expect the material to assist the defence, making answer A incorrect. Answer B is incorrect as Paragraph 5.16 of the Disclosure Manual makes observations concerning negative results/information and although it does not provide a precise definition, it will include the result of an inquiry that differs from what might be expected, given the prevailing circumstances. A finger-mark from a crime scene that cannot be identified as belonging to a known suspect is one such example of 'negative information'. Although this does not identify the suspect, it casts doubt on the suspect's guilt, or implicates another person and as such it should be disclosed. Section 7A of the Act states that the fact that the prosecution has made secondary disclosure does not relieve them of the continuing duty to disclose at any time between the initial disclosure and the accused being acquitted or convicted or the prosecutor deciding not to proceed with the case concerned, making answer D incorrect.

Evidence and Procedure, paras 2.9.4.2, 2.9.4.8, 2.9.4.9

29. Answer **B** — When GRASTER enters the house initially he commits a burglary contrary to s. 9(1)(a) but as he has no weapon of offence, firearm, imitation firearm or explosive with him at the time it is not an aggravated burglary. The moment he picks up the letter opener to stab someone it becomes a weapon of offence but at this stage the aggravated offence has not been committed as he did not enter with the weapon (so no aggravated 9(1)(a) burglary) and although he has entered as a trespasser he has not, as yet, stolen, committed grievous bodily harm or attempted to do so (so no aggravated 9(1)(b)), making answer A incorrect. As soon as GRASTER steals the £200.00 he commits the 9(1)(b) offence and at the time has with him a weapon of offence so the aggravated offence is committed at this point (answer B). This makes answers C and D incorrect.

Crime, paras 1.12.3 to 1.12.4.1

30. Answer **B** — Section 3(1) of the Act provides that this offence can be committed by publishing a statement on the Internet (the most likely place that it will be published!), making answer A incorrect. The maximum term of imprisonment is seven years, making answer C incorrect. The offence can be committed outside the United Kingdom and requires the consent of the DPP to prosecute, making answer D incorrect.

General Police Duties, para. 4.6.14.5

31. Answer **A** — The maximum period that a parenting order will last is for a period not exceeding 12 months.

Evidence and Procedure, para. 2.6.7

32. Answer **B** — There is no particular rank required to run a first stage meeting, all that is required is that the individual is a 'line manager', making answer A incorrect. If an improvement notice is issued to the officer then its 'specified period' (a period specified by the line manager conducting the first meeting within which the police officer must improve his/her performance) would not normally exceed three months. However, depending on the nature and circumstances of the matter, it may be appropriate to specify a longer or shorter period for improvement (but which should not exceed 12 months), making answer C incorrect. A police officer does have a right of appeal against any

improvement notice imposed at a first stage meeting, making answer D incorrect. A line manager can ask a human resources professional or a police officer (who should have experience of UPPs and be independent of the line management chain) to attend a UPP meeting to advise him/her on the proceedings at the first stage meeting.

VERIFICATION QUESTION, *General Police Duties*, paras 4.1.17.8, 4.1.17.15

33. Answer **D** — When COSGRIFF threatens BURNELL in the car he commits an assault. This is because the threat is an immediate one conditional upon some real circumstance (*Read* v *Coker* (1853) 13 CB 850). This makes answers A and C incorrect. An assault is not committed when the threat is made in the presence of the police officer because the threat is a conditional one (*Tuberville* v *Savage* (1669) 1 Mod 3), making answer B incorrect.

Crime, para. 1.7.2.3

34. Answer **A** — The power under s. 60 of the Criminal Justice and Public Order Act 1994 can be authorised by an officer of the rank of inspector or above, making answer D incorrect. The initial maximum period that it may be authorised for must not exceed 24 hours, making answer C incorrect. Section 60(1)(aa) states that the power can be authorised if an incident of serious violence has taken place in England and Wales in the authorising officer's area, that a dangerous instrument or offensive weapon used in the incident is being carried in the locality in his police area by a person and that it is expedient to give an authorisation to find the instrument or weapon, making answer B incorrect. When the power is authorised by an inspector, a superintendent must be informed of the decision as soon as practicable.

General Police Duties, para. 4.4.4.12

35. Answer **D** — Answer A is incorrect as misconduct in a public office can be committed by omission. Answer B is incorrect as a purely personal matter arising while the officer was off duty would not normally mean the offence has been committed. This is because the offence is concerned with conduct/omission involving a public office holder who is *acting as such*. Answer C is incorrect: simple inadvertence or an accidental action/omission will not be enough to commit the offence which relates to wilful neglect and/or wilful misconduct. Answers A, B and C relate to the case of *Attorney-General's Reference (No. 3 of 2003)* [2004] EWCA Crim 868). The sentence for this offence is imprisonment 'at large', meaning there is no limit relating to the length of sentence.

General Police Duties, para. 4.1.21.1

36. Answer **B** — This question requires you to consider what 'violence' is under the Public Order Act 1986. Section 8 of the Act states that 'violence' will include violent conduct against property as well as violent conduct towards persons (except in the context of affray). It also states that 'violence' is not restricted to conduct causing or intended to cause injury or damage but includes any other violent conduct (for example, throwing at or towards a person a missile of a kind capable of causing injury which does not hit or falls short). All of the participants in this question have therefore used or threatened violence. However, under s. 1 of the Act, the threat or use of violence must be unlawful and STRACHAN's use of violence was in self-defence so it would not be unlawful; STRACHAN does not commit the offence and so answers C and D are incorrect. Answer D is also incorrect as, although 12 or more persons must threaten or use unlawful violence, it is only those actually *using*

violence who are guilty of the offence. The definition of violence means that LAKE, McNAB and NISBET commit the offence, making answer A incorrect.

General Police Duties, paras 4.6.4, 4.6.4.1

37. Answer **B** — Code C, paragraph 2.4 details the rights of an appropriate adult to consult the custody record. A solicitor and/or appropriate adult must be permitted to consult a detainee's custody record as soon as practicable after their arrival at the police station and at any other time whilst the person is detained. Arrangements for access must be agreed with the custody officer and may not unreasonably interfere with the custody officer's duties.

Evidence and Procedure, para. 2.10.5

38. Answer **C** — Section 7 of the Bail Act 1976 provides three occasions when a constable may arrest a person released on bail: (i) if the constable has reasonable grounds for believing that the person is not likely to surrender to custody; (ii) if the constable has reasonable grounds for believing that the person is likely to break any of the conditions of his bail or has reasonable grounds for suspecting that the person has broken any of those conditions; or (iii) in a case where that person was released on bail with one or more surety or sureties, if a surety notifies a constable in writing that the person is unlikely to surrender to custody and for that reason the surety wishes to be relieved of his obligations as a surety. Answers B and D are incorrect as the Act provides three grounds for arrest and not one. Answer A is incorrect because the notification must be made in writing.

Evidence and Procedure, para. 2.4.7.4

39. Answer **C** — There are two 'lawful excuses' detailed in the Criminal Damage Act 1971, they are permission and protection. Just because BURDOCK did not act to protect the property will not deprive him of the potential to say that he acted with the permission of a relevant person, making answer A incorrect. Section 5(2) of the Act states that a person will be treated as having a 'lawful excuse' to commit criminal damage if at the time of the act or acts alleged to constitute the offence (*when BURDOCK damages the grilles*) he believed that the person or persons whom he believed to be entitled to consent to the destruction of or damage to the property in question had so consented (*he believed CAIN consented*), or would have consented to it if he or they had known of the destruction or damage and its circumstances. Such a belief need only be honestly held. This makes answer D incorrect. There is no limitation regarding the amount of damage caused, making answer B incorrect.

Crime, para. 1.14.2.6

40. Answer **C** — Section 12 of the Public Order Act 1986 allows for conditions to be imposed on public processions. These conditions may be imposed by 'the senior police officer'. For the purposes of s. 12, the 'senior police officer' is:

- in relation to a procession being held or intended to be held where people are assembling to take part in it, the most senior officer present at the scene;
- in relation to any other intended procession, the chief officer of police.

Therefore, where advance notice of a procession is given, the chief of police may impose conditions on the procession. Where the procession has already begun, or where people are gathering to take part in it, the most senior officer present at the scene may impose conditions.

General Police Duties, para. 4.6.11.3

41. Answer **A** — The right under s. 56 of the Police and Criminal Evidence Act 1984 may be delayed if authorised by an officer of the rank of inspector or above (making answers C and D incorrect). The maximum period that the right can be delayed is 36 hours (making answer B incorrect).

Evidence and Procedure, para. 2.10.6.2

42. Answer **B** — Answer A is incorrect as when giving testimony in a witness statement used as per the Criminal Justice Act 1967, i.e. an MG9, then that person commits the offence of providing a false statement under oath (contrary to s. 2 of the Perjury Act 1911) and not perjury. Answer D is incorrect as TOLDAN *does* commit an offence of perjury— this is at point B (although answer C would be a further offence of perjury). Perjury is committed when a person who is lawfully sworn as a witness in judicial proceedings wilfully makes a statement which is material to the proceedings and that person knows to be false or does not believe to be true. 'Judicial proceedings' includes courts or tribunals.

Crime, para. 1.15.2

43. Answer **C** — There is a defence to the offence of being in charge of a mechanically propelled vehicle whilst unfit through drink or drugs under s. 4(3) of the Road Traffic Act 1988, making answer A incorrect. The defence states that the person will not be deemed to be in charge of the mechanically propelled vehicle if he/she can prove that at the material time the circumstances were such that there was no likelihood of him/her driving the vehicle so long as they remained unfit to drive through drink or drugs. However, in determining whether the defendant was likely to drive the vehicle, a court may disregard any injury to the defendant or damage to the vehicle (s. 4(4) of the Act), making answers B and D incorrect.

Road Policing, para. 3.5.2

44. Answer **B** — The offence of people trafficking is committed when a person:

- arranges or facilitates the arrival in, or entry into, the United Kingdom of an individual (the 'passenger') and he intends to exploit that passenger in the United Kingdom or elsewhere or he believes that another person is likely to exploit the passenger in the United Kingdom or elsewhere (HUNT);
- arranges or facilitates travel within the United Kingdom by an individual (the 'passenger') in respect of whom he believes that an offence as above may have been committed (PLANT) and he intends to exploit that passenger in the United Kingdom or elsewhere or he believes that another person is likely to exploit the passenger in the United Kingdom or elsewhere;
- arranges or facilitates the departure from the United Kingdom of an individual (the 'passenger') (FINCH) and he intends to exploit that passenger outside the United Kingdom or elsewhere or he believes that another person is likely to exploit the passenger outside the United Kingdom.

It does not matter what country the 'passenger' comes from.

VERIFICATION QUESTION, *Crime*, para. 1.16.3.3

45. Answer **D** — A shotgun is a smooth-bore gun, making answers A and C incorrect. The smooth-bore gun will be a shotgun if it has a barrel not less than 24 inches in length, making answer B incorrect.

General Police Duties, para. 4.7.4.3

46. Answer **D** — The Criminal Justice and Immigration Act 2008 has made certain amendments to s. 11 of the 1980 Magistrates' Courts Act regarding proceeding to trial in the absence of the accused. Where the accused has attained the age of 18, the court *must* proceed in his/her absence unless it appears to the court that this would be contrary to the interests of justice to do so (s. 11(1)(b)). This makes answers A and B incorrect. The court is not required to enquire into the reasons for the accused's failure to appear (s. 11(6)), making answer C incorrect. Where a court imposes a custodial sentence in the absence of the accused, the accused must be brought before the court before commencing the custodial sentence (s. 11(3A)).

Evidence and Procedure, para. 2.5.6

47. Answer **B** — The rest period may be interrupted if Code C, para. 12.2 applies. This includes several reasons for interrupting an interview apart from that cited at answer A (making answer A incorrect). Paragraph 12.2 states that the rest period can be interrupted at the request of the detainee, their appropriate adult or legal representative (making answer C incorrect). Answer D is incorrect as no authorisation level is mentioned in the Codes of Practice. If the detainee requests that the rest period be interrupted then a fresh rest period is not required (Code C, para. 12.2).

Evidence and Procedure, para. 2.12.9.2

48. Answer **B** — In *R v Loosely; Attorney General's Reference (No. 3) of 2000* [2001] 1 WLR 2060, the House of Lords stated that if the police did no more than present a person with an 'unexceptional opportunity' to commit a criminal offence and that person took that opportunity, it would not amount to an abuse of process.

Crime, paras 1.3.6.1 to 1.3.6.2

49. Answer **A** — The requirement for the power under s. 1 of the Act to be used is that a constable reasonably *suspects* that he/she will find stolen or prohibited articles, articles falling under s. 139 of the Criminal Justice Act 1988 (bladed or sharply pointed articles) or any firework to which subsection 8B applies, making answer D incorrect. Section 1(4) of the Act states that if a person is in a garden or yard occupied with and used for the purposes of dwelling or on other land so occupied and used, a constable may not search him in the exercise of the power conferred by this section unless the constable has reasonable grounds for believing:

(a) that he does not reside in the dwelling; and
(b) that he is not in the place in question with the express or implied permission of a person who resides in the dwelling.

Both person and vehicle may be searched if these conditions are satisfied, making answers B and C incorrect.

General Police Duties, paras 4.4.4.2 to 4.4.4.5

50. Answer **C** — Section 40 of the Police and Criminal Evidence Act 1984 requires that a person who has been refused bail must have his/her detention reviewed by the custody officer within nine hours of the last decision to refuse bail.

Evidence and Procedure, para. 2.4.10.1

51. Answer **C** — The state of mind required to prove an offence of handling stolen goods is that the defendant knew or believed the goods to be stolen goods. THACKERY has no idea that the watch is stolen and so cannot be guilty of the offence. Answer A is incorrect as the provisions of the Act apply whether the stealing took place in England or Wales or elsewhere (e.g. France), provided that the stealing amounted to an offence where and when the goods were stolen. Answer B is incorrect as the watch will always be 'stolen goods', even in the hands of an innocent person unless they have been restored to the person from whom they were originally stolen or to other lawful possession or custody or after that person and any other person claiming through him otherwise ceased as regards those goods to have any right to restitution in respect of the theft (s. 24(3)). Answer D is incorrect as the term 'stolen property' includes any goods which directly or indirectly represent the stolen goods in the hands of the thief (s. 24(2)(a)).

Crime, paras 1.12.16 to 1.12.16.1

52. Answer **A** — The Standards of Professional Behaviour apply to police officers of all ranks from chief constable to constable, special constables and to those subject to suspension.

VERIFICATION QUESTION, *General Police Duties*, para. 4.1.9

53. Answer **A** — A significant statement is one that appears capable of being used in evidence against a suspect, particularly a direct admission of guilt (Code C, para. 11.4A). A significant statement can be made at any time, meaning that answers B and D are incorrect. Answer C is incorrect as the significant statement should be put to the suspect at the start of the interview.

Evidence and Procedure, para. 2.12.9.8

54. Answer **B** — A final warning can be given on more than one occasion, making answer A incorrect. There is no requirement in respect of the nature of the offence being different on the second occasion, making answer C incorrect, neither is there a requirement to consult with the CPS before the warning is issued, making answer D incorrect. A second final warning can be given where the offender has been previously warned, the offence was committed more than two years after the date of the previous warning and the constable considers the offence to be not so serious as to require a charge to be brought.

Evidence and Procedure, paras 2.6.7.1 to 2.6.7.2

55. Answer **A** — This offence replaced the deception element of the offence of going equipped (s. 25 of the Theft Act 1968). The offence is committed if a person has anything in his/her possession or control (as ALDINGTON does when he picks up the identification card) for use in the course of or in connection with any fraud. The offence can be committed anywhere so is complete when ALDINGTON takes possession of the identification card in the hallway. Possession can be to enable another to commit an offence of fraud.

Crime, para. 1.13.7

56. Answer **C** — The power under s. 136 of the Mental Health Act 1983 does not need the presence of a medical professional in order to be used, making answer D incorrect. Section 138 provides that a person removed to a place of safety under s. 136 or a person removed under a warrant, who subsequently escapes while being taken to or detained in a place of safety, cannot generally be

retaken after 72 hours have elapsed. This means that both LERWICK and DRAY can be retaken, and makes answers A and B incorrect.

Crime, paras 1.9.12.1 to 1.9.12.3

57. Answer **C** — The offence of child abduction under s. 2 of the 1984 Act is committed when, without lawful authority or reasonable excuse, a person takes or detains a child under the age of 16 so as to remove him from the lawful control of any person having lawful control of the child or so as to keep him out of the lawful control of any person entitled to lawful control of the child. There is no requirement under s. 2 of the Act for the child to be taken or sent out of the United Kingdom, making answer D incorrect. The fact that the child consented to the taking etc. and that no force was used is immaterial, making answer B incorrect. However, PARSON would have a defence if he can prove that at the time of the alleged offence, he believed, on reasonable grounds, that he was the child's father (s. 2(3)(a) of the Act). The fact that PARSON and MILLER were not married and PARSON is not actually the father of the child will not preclude the use of the defence.

Crime, paras 1.11.3.3 to 1.11.3.4

58. Answer **B** — The premises must be occupied or controlled by the arrested person. This expression is not defined but it is a *factual* requirement, i.e. it is not enough that the officer suspects or believes that the premises are occupied or controlled by that person. This makes answers C and D incorrect. Answer D is additionally incorrect as the search can only take place if the officer has reasonable grounds to suspect that there is (on the premises) evidence that relates to (a) that offence, or (b) to some other indictable offence and not merely because the person arrested has been arrested for an indictable offence. Answer A is incorrect as the search can take place at premises occupied or controlled by the person under arrest.

General Police Duties, para. 4.4.13.1

59. Answer **D** — Once a detainee has been seen by the health-care professional any clinical directions and advice, including any further clarifications, given to police by the health-care professional concerning the care and treatment of the detainee must be recorded in the custody record, making answer B incorrect. However, this does not require the health-care professional to record his/her clinical findings in the custody record. Information about the cause of any injury, ailment or condition does not need to be recorded in the custody record if it appears capable of providing evidence of the offence, making answer A incorrect and answer D correct. Answer C is incorrect as the authorisation to record such information elsewhere does not require the authorisation of an inspector.

Evidence and Procedure, para. 2.10.11.18

60. Answer **D** — The offence of exposure is committed if a person intentionally exposes their genitals and they intend that someone will see them and be caused alarm or distress. Exposing the buttocks or the breasts will not amount to an offence under this section.

Crime, para. 1.9.8.1

61. Answer **B** — Section 1 of the Criminal Procedure and Investigations Act 1996 defines in which type of cases the disclosure provisions apply. In reality this *applies to all cases* other than those where the defendant pleads 'guilty' at the magistrates' court. This makes answers A, C and D incorrect.

Evidence and Procedure, para. 2.9.4.1

62. Answer **C** — The Serious Organised Crime and Police Act 2005 added an additional section to this offence (s. 3A) specifically designed to protect employees and companies against the activities of animal rights activists. The fact that HARKER's conduct is aimed at two people rather than one is immaterial, making answer A incorrect. Although companies and corporations could not apply for injunctions in the past, the new section (s. 3A) allows this to take place, making answer B incorrect. Answer D is incorrect as a 'course of conduct' may mean, in the case of conduct in relation to two or more people, conduct on at least one occasion in relation to each of these people.

General Police Duties, para. 4.5.5.1

63. Answer **A** — A parenting order may be made against one or both biological parents (this could include a father who may not be married to the mother) or a person who is a guardian of the child.

Evidence and Procedure, para. 2.6.7.3

64. Answer **A** — Careless or inconsiderate driving under s. 3 of the Road Traffic Act 1988 is an offence committed by the use of a mechanically propelled vehicle and not a motor vehicle, making answer B incorrect. Evidence of earlier incidents involving careless or inconsiderate driving around the same time as the offence charged may be admissible to support the charge under some circumstances (*Hallet* v *Warren* (1926) 93 JP 225) as it may if the offence is charged as one continuing offence (*Horrix* v *Malam* [1984] RTR 112), making answer C incorrect. In order to prove that a driver drove inconsiderately you must show that some other person using the road was actually inconvenienced (*Dilks* v *Bowman-Shaw* [1981] RTR 4). Other persons using the road/public place can include pedestrians who are deliberately sprayed with water from a puddle or passengers in a vehicle (see *Pawley* v *Wharldall* [1966] 1 QB 373) therefore answer D is incorrect.

Road Policing, paras 3.2.4 to 3.2.4.2

65. Answer **B** — Although this offence can be committed with an imitation firearm as well as a real firearm, the House of Lords have overturned a decision which allowed a defendant's use of his stiffened fingers beneath his coat to qualify as an imitation firearm for the purposes of this offence (*R* v *Bentham* [2005] UKHL 18), making answer A incorrect. Schedule 1 offences are committed when the defendant has a firearm or imitation firearm in their possession at the time of the commission of the offence or of being arrested for an offence (not necessarily the one that was committed with the firearm or imitation firearm). The offences that relate to Schedule 1 follow the mnemonic DART, the R of which signifies the offence of rape and several other sexual offences. Therefore, at point B, HOLTHAM commits the offence, making answer D incorrect. Answer C is further incorrect as s. 18 wounding is not a Schedule 1 offence.

General Police Duties, para. 4.7.8.4

66. Answer **D** — The folding pocket knife in HAYWARD's possession would not be classed as a bladed or pointed instrument; the cutting edge of the blade would have to exceed 3 inches (7.62 cm) for it to be caught by the Act. This makes answers A and C incorrect. The dagger in GLENN's possession would be classed as a bladed or pointed article. However, 'school premises' means land used for the purposes of a school and excludes any land occupied solely as a dwelling by any person employed at the school. This means that the provisions would not apply to someone found in the garden of a caretaker's house if the house was occupied solely as a dwelling by the school caretaker.

General Police Duties, para. 4.8.4

67. Answer **C** — Regulation 107 prohibits the leaving of an *unattended* motor vehicle on a road unless the engine has been stopped *and* the brake set. Any person left 'attending' the vehicle must be someone who is licensed to drive it and in a position to intervene otherwise reg. 107 is breached. POTTER has not committed the offence, making answer A incorrect. GUNNER does not need to be in the driver's seat, just in a position to intervene, making answer B incorrect. Purely having the brake set would not mean that the offences has not been committed, making D incorrect.

Road Policing, para. 3.9.4.5

68. Answer **A** — A s. 9(1)(a) burglary is committed when a person enters a building or part of a building as a trespasser with the intention of committing theft (s. 1 of the Theft Act 1968), grievous bodily harm (s. 18 of the Offences Against the Person Act 1861) or criminal damage (s. 1(1) of the Criminal Damage Act 1971). Section 47 assault and kidnapping have never been part of the definition making answers B and D incorrect. Rape was removed from the definition as a consequence of the 2003 Sexual Offences Act, making answer C incorrect.

Crime, para. 1.12.3.3

69. Answer **D** — Section 3(7) of the Bail Act 1976 states that a parent or guardian may act as a surety for a child or young person, making answers A and B incorrect. However, such a requirement cannot be imposed on the parent or guardian where it appears that the young person will have attained the age of 17 before the time to be appointed for him to surrender to custody (not 14 as in answer C which is incorrect). No parent or guardian shall be bound to a sum greater than £50.00 (s. 3(7)(b)).

VERIFICATION QUESTION, *Evidence and Procedure*, para. 2.4.7.1

70. Answer **B** — This offence is punishable with a maximum of five years' imprisonment, making answer D incorrect. There is no requirement as to the actual consequences of a defendant's actions under s. 24 of the Offences Against the Person Act 1861 as the offence is concerned with the defendant's intentions, making answer A incorrect. Answer C is incorrect as, although MITCHAM did not intend to injure JAMIL, the offence can be committed when the defendant intends to injure, aggrieve or annoy another person.

Crime, para. 1.8.3.1

71. Answer **B** — Duress of circumstances applies where the defendant has been compelled to act as he/she did or face serious injury or death. The defence will apply to offences of careless and inconsiderate driving, making answers A and C incorrect. It will also apply to an offence of driving a motor vehicle whilst over the prescribed limit (*DPP* v *Bell* [1992] RTR 335), making answer D incorrect.

Road Policing, para. 3.2.13

72. Answer **C** — Answer A is incorrect as confession evidence can be excluded under s. 78 as well as s. 76 of the Police and Criminal Evidence Act 1984. Answer B is incorrect as evidence can also be excluded under s. 82(1) of the Act that preserves the court's common law power to exclude evidence at its discretion. Answer D is incorrect as once the defence raise the issue of oppression or unreliability it is for the prosecution to prove the confession was not obtained in such circumstances (*R* v *Allen*, 10 July 2001 (CA), unreported). The burden of proof will be beyond all reasonable doubt.

Evidence and Procedure, paras 2.8.1, 2.8.2.1, 2.8.3.2

73. Answer **C** — The offence under s. 3 of the Football (Offences) Act 1991 is committed when a person takes part in chanting which is of an indecent or racialist nature at a designated football match. Answer A is incorrect as 'chanting' means the repeated uttering of any words or sounds. Answer B is incorrect as the chanting can be by an individual or in concert with one or more others. The term 'racialist' requires that the chanting is threatening, abusive or insulting to a person by reason of his/ her colour, race, nationality (including citizenship) or ethnic or national origins. In *DPP* v *Stoke on Trent Magistrates' Court* [2003] 3 All ER 1086, the Administrative Court held that shouting the phrase used in the question at supporters from Oldham fell squarely within the definition.

General Police Duties, para. 4.6.13.1

74. Answer **D** — The 'gain' for the purposes of blackmail includes a gain by keeping what one has. This would be the case with KNOTT who keeps the compensation money instead of paying it to JALOTA, making answer A incorrect. Answer B is incorrect as there is no such offence as an attempted blackmail. The offence is either committed or it is not. The offence, when committed by letter, is similar to contract law; that is when you post the demand (as with contracts) the offence is complete, making answer B incorrect. The words used in the letter may not be 'menaces' that would intimidate or influence the average person but if a threat bears a particular significance for the victim (as in the question) that will be enough, provided the defendant was aware of the fact. This last point makes answer C incorrect.

Crime, paras 1.12.10 to 1.12.10.2

75. Answer **D** — The fact that the consent to sexual intercourse was obtained by a false promise of marriage does not make PARK guilty of rape, making answer C incorrect. BYTON has consented to sexual intercourse— she was not deceived as to the nature of the act, making answer A incorrect. Violence need not be used or threatened for rape to take place, making answer B incorrect.

Crime, paras 1.9.3 to 1.9.3.4

76. Answer **B** — An ASBO has a minimum period of two years' duration (Crime and Disorder Act 1998, s. 1(7)).

General Police Duties, para. 4.5.6.6

77. Answer **A** — This is an offence of intent. The intent can be one of four types and one of those four is an intention to cause economic loss to any person by reason of goods being shunned by members of the public. This makes answer B incorrect. The fact that sales are unaffected is immaterial, making answer D incorrect. The term 'goods' includes natural and manufactured goods, so that compact discs and DVDs would be covered by the legislation (s. 38(5)).

Crime, para. 1.14.8

78. Answer **C** — Section 20 of the Act requires a wounding *or* a grievous bodily harm, making answer A incorrect. The fact that the women consented to sexual intercourse will not preclude the conviction of GARBUT as per the ruling in *R* v *Konzani* [2005] EWCA Crim 706, where the court held that there was a critical distinction between taking the risk as to the various potentially adverse (and possibly problematic) consequences of unprotected consensual sexual intercourse and the giving of informed consent to the risk of infection with a fatal disease (making answer B incorrect). There is no

requirement for the prosecution to prove intent (this relates to s. 18 of the Act) and consequently, answer D is incorrect.

Crime, para. 1.7.6.2

79. Answer **B** — For a reportable accident to occur the mechanically propelled vehicle must be present on a road or public place. That is the case when SWAN drives the BMW off the private land and on to a road. The BMW will still be on a road as it drives through the gate onto KENNETT's land. An accident occurs under s. 170(1)(iii) of the Act when damage is caused to any property constructed on, fixed to, growing in or otherwise forming part of the land on which the road or place in question is situated *or land adjacent to such land*. This makes answer A incorrect. Neither hitting the water-trough or the injuries caused to KENNETT are reportable accident matters — they occurred on private land.

Road Policing, para. 3.4.2

80. Answer **D** — Whether there has been a road accident or not does not affect the fact that there is a power of entry to arrest for this offence (under s. 17(c)(iiia) of the Police and Criminal Evidence Act 1984, making answer A incorrect. As there is a power of entry, answer C is incorrect. An officer does not have to be in uniform to arrest a person for an offence under s. 4(1) of the Road Traffic Act 1988, neither do they have to be in uniform to exercise the power of entry, making answer B incorrect.

Road Policing, para. 3.5.2

81. Answer **D** — An offence under s. 1A of the Sporting Events (Control of Alcohol) Act 1985 is committed when a vehicle (not being a public service vehicle) is used to carry two or more passengers for the whole or part of a journey to a designated sporting event. A person will commit an offence if he/she knowingly causes or permits intoxicating liquor to be carried on the vehicle if he/she is the driver, the keeper or the servant or agent of its keeper and also if he/she is drunk in such a motor vehicle. However, the vehicle must be adapted to carry *more than* eight passengers. Therefore, answers A, B and C are incorrect as no offence is committed.

VERIFICATION QUESTION, *General Police Duties*, paras 4.6.13.8, 4.6.13.9

82. Answer **A** — The House of Lords has held that, in order to prove the offence of affray, the threat of unlawful violence has to be towards a person(s) present at the scene (*I v DPP* [2002] 1 AC 285). Therefore, if there is nobody to whom the unlawful violence is being threatened there can be no affray.

General Police Duties, para. 4.6.6

83. Answer **D** — The offence under s. 63 is committed when a person is a trespasser on any premises, he intends to commit a relevant sexual offence on the premises and he knows that, or is reckless as to whether, he is a trespasser. It should be noted that this offence is only committed when the relevant sexual offence is going to be carried out in the premises where the offender is a trespasser. As STATEN is not going to commit a sexual offence when he trespasses in the tent, the offence is not committed at points A or B. It is not committed at point C as STATEN is not a trespasser in his own motor home vehicle.

Crime, para. 1.9.9.2

84. Answer **B** — A failure to follow the Codes of Practice is not an automatic reason for excluding evidence, making answer D incorrect. Answer C is incorrect as the oppression must have been against the person who makes the confession. Answer A is incorrect as there can be 'oppressive' behaviour even though the Codes of Practice have been followed.

Evidence and Procedure, para. 2.8.2.3

85. Answer **C** — Answer A is incorrect as PURCELL does not have to act for gain for the offence to be committed. Answer B is incorrect as you must show that the defendant knew or had reasonable cause for believing that his/her act facilitated the commission of the breach of immigration law *and* also that the person was not an EU citizen. Answer D is incorrect as this offence can be committed outside the United Kingdom by British citizens and others with relevant forms of citizenship (Immigration Act 1971, s. 25(5)).

Crime, para. 1.16.3.1

86. Answer **C** — To prove the offence of allowing to be carried (under s. 12 of the Theft Act 1968) you must be able to show that a defendant allowed himself/herself to be carried in or on the conveyance, that the defendant knew the conveyance had been taken without the required consent or authority and that there was some movement of the conveyance while the defendant was in it (*R v Diggin* (1980) 72 Cr App R 204).

Crime, para. 1.11.6.3

87. Answer **C** — An individual taken to a designated place under this section may be detained there until the end of 48 hours from the time of his arrest (s. 5(3)).

General Police Duties, para. 4.6.15

88. Answer **A** — A preliminary breath test can only be administered at or near the place where the requirement to co-operate with the test is imposed, making answer B incorrect. Answer C is incorrect as a preliminary impairment test can be carried out at a police station if the constable making the requirement thinks it expedient (as per answer A). Answer D is incorrect as the constable administering the test under s. 6 of the Road Traffic Act 1988 must be in uniform (unless the test is administered after an accident (s. 6(5) of the Act)).

Road Policing, para. 3.5.4.2

89. Answer **D** — Section 54A of the Police and Criminal Evidence Act 1984 (as inserted by the Anti-terrorism, Crime and Security Act 2001) provides a power to search and/or examine detained persons without their consent. This must be in order to ascertain whether the person has any mark that would tend to identify him/her as a person involved in the commission of an offence or to assist to identify him/her. Mark includes features and injuries. The search/examination is authorised by an officer of at least the rank of inspector. Authorisation may be given orally or in writing but if given orally it must be confirmed in writing as soon as possible.

Evidence and Procedure, para. 2.10.12.1

90. Answer **C** — Where a constable in uniform requires a person driving a motor vehicle to stop the vehicle (as per s. 163 of the Road Traffic Act 1988) and that person fails to stop the vehicle, or to stop the vehicle for long enough, for the constable to make such lawful enquiries as he/she considers

appropriate and the constable has reasonable grounds for *believing* that the vehicle is or was being driven without insurance then he/she may seize the vehicle. PC KHAN only *suspects* so the power is not available (answer D is incorrect). The fact that the car is in a garage next to a house would not stop the use of the power in the right circumstances (answer A). There is no requirement for a witness to the seizure should the powers be used (answer B).

Road Policing, para. 3.6.2.7

91. Answer **A** — Answer D is incorrect as the seriousness of the offence alone has been deemed not to be sufficient reason to suppose a person will necessarily abscond (*Yagci and Sargin* v *Turkey* (1995) 20 EHRR 505), and regard *must* be taken of other factors including the character of the detained person, their background, financial status, etc. (*RW* v *Switzerland* (1994) 17 EHRR 60). If a detained person has previously been bailed and there was no evidence of interference with the course of justice, using this ground would be very difficult to justify (*Ringeisen* v *Austria* (1979–80) 1 EHRR 455), making answer B incorrect. It was held in *Matznetter* v *Austria* (1979–80) 1 EHRR 198 and *Toth* v *Austria* (1992) 14 EHRR 551 that a reasonable risk of the detained person committing further offences whilst on bail was a valid reason for refusal of bail, making answer C incorrect. *Letellier* v *France* (1992) 14 EHRR 83 provides for the temporary detention of a person where the particular gravity of the offence(s) and the likely public reaction is that the release may give rise to public disorder.

VERIFICATION QUESTION, *Evidence and Procedure*, paras 2.4.16 to 2.4.16.4

92. Answer **B** — Article 15 of the Human Rights Convention states that in times of war or other public emergency threatening the life of the nation a nation may take measures to derogate from its obligations under the Convention. However, no derogations from Article 2, except in respect of deaths resulting from the lawful acts of war, or from Articles 3, 4 and 7 shall be made. The prohibition of torture is absolute and, irrespective of the prevailing circumstances, there can be no derogation from an individual's absolute right to freedom from torture. This makes answers A and C incorrect. Answer C is additionally incorrect as the derogation made by the United Kingdom under the Anti-terrorism, Crime and Security Act 2001 relates to permitting the longer detention of terrorist suspects before charge. Answer D is incorrect, as torture has been classed as inhuman treatment resulting in intense suffering, both physical and mental and degrading treatment giving rise to fear and anguish in the victim, causing feelings of inferiority and humiliation.

General Police Duties, paras 4.3.6, 4.3.14

93. Answer **A** — The activities of both CUTHBERT and FRANCIS seem to fall into the category of harbouring a person as they have, respectively, provided AUSTIN with shelter and given assistance with intent to hinder or interfere with his being taken into custody. However, s. 22(2) of the Criminal Justice Act 1961 does not apply to a prisoner who escapes while in transit to or from prison (*R* v *Moss* (1985) 82 Cr App R 116).

Crime, para. 1.15.9

94. Answer **C** — Answer A is incorrect as this offence applies to a 'mechanically propelled vehicle' and includes quad bikes. Answer B is incorrect as the driving of the defendant must be shown to be *a* cause of death; it is not necessary to show that it was the sole or even substantial cause of death (*R* v *Hennigan* [1971] 3 All ER 133). Therefore it is irrelevant whether or not the person killed contributed to the incident which resulted in his/her death. Answer D is incorrect as the test in relation to

whether driving was dangerous is an objective one, i.e. if the driving were dangerous and this would be obvious to a competent and careful driver.

Road Policing, paras 3.2.2 to 3.2.2.2

95. Answer **D** — Code C, para. 6.5A states that if an appropriate adult requests legal advice but the detained juvenile does not wish to consult the solicitor, he/she cannot be forced to speak to the solicitor. Answer A is incorrect as a 'solicitor' for the purposes of the Codes of Practice includes a trainee solicitor. Answer B is incorrect as if a solicitor arrives at a police station to see a suspect, the suspect must be asked whether he/she would like to see the solicitor *regardless of what legal advice has already been received* (Code C, para. 6.15). If the investigating officer considers that a solicitor is acting in such a way that he/she cannot properly put questions to a suspect, he/she will stop the interview and consult an officer not below the rank of superintendent, if one is readily available, otherwise an officer not below the rank of inspector who is not connected with the investigation, to decide whether that solicitor should be excluded from the interview (Code C, para. 6.10) therefore answer C is incorrect.

Evidence and Procedure, para. 2.12.9.13

96. Answer **D** — The prescribed limit in relation to urine is 107 milligrammes of alcohol in 100 millilitres of urine, making answer A incorrect. Answer B is incorrect as the choice of what sample (blood or urine) to provide in such circumstances is made by the officer (s. 7(4) of the Road Traffic Act 1988). When specimens of breath have not been provided elsewhere and at the time the requirement is made a device or a reliable device is not available at the police station, a requirement for a specimen of blood or urine can be made at a police station (s. 7(3)(b) of the Act) making answer C incorrect.

Road Policing, paras 3.5.3, 3.5.5.1, 3.5.5.7

97. Answer **B** — Section 21 provides that where a person has been sentenced to imprisonment, youth custody, detention in a young offenders' institution or a secure training order for three months or more, but less than three years, they must not have a firearm or ammunition in their possession for a period of five years beginning on the date of their release. If the person has been sentenced to custody for life or to preventive detention, imprisonment, corrective training, youth custody or detention in a young offender institution for three years or more they must not at any time have a firearm or ammunition in their possession.

General Police Duties, para. 4.7.9

98. Answer **B** — If medical treatment leads to a victim's death, that will not normally be regarded as a 'new' act (*R* v *Smith* (1959) 2 QB 35), making answer A incorrect. The actions of a victim attempting to escape a serious sexual assault by jumping from a car would not break the chain of causation unless they were done entirely of the victim's own volition or where they are 'daft', making answer C incorrect. Answer D is incorrect as drug dealers are not generally liable for the deaths of their victims as death is brought about by the deliberate exercise of free will by the drug user.

Crime, para. 1.2.5

99. Answer **A** — HAMPSHIRE does not commit the offence of theft because when he took the mobile phone from O'SHEA he believed he had a right in law to do so and therefore he will not be dishonest. This makes answers B and C incorrect. HAMPSHIRE does commit the offence of re-programming a

mobile phone, making answer D incorrect. The offence can be committed in a variety of ways, one of which is by changing the unique device identifier on a mobile phone. The fact that HAMPSHIRE is in lawful possession of the mobile phone makes no difference as the only defence to this activity is if the person changes the unique device identifier and he is the manufacturer of the device or he does so with the written consent of the manufacturer of the device.

Crime, paras 1.12.2.1, 1.12.15

100. Answer **A** — A wife, husband or civil partner is only compellable to give evidence on behalf of the prosecution in certain circumstances. Answer B is not one of those as the sexual offence the wife has witnessed would need to be committed on a person who at the time of the offence was *under* 16 years of age. C is wrong as once again the victim of the assault/injury would need to be under 16 years of age at the material time. Answer D is incorrect as theft is not an offence covered by this legislation.

Evidence and Procedure, para. 2.5.8.6

101. Answer **B** — If impressions of a person's footwear are to be taken at a police station with that person's consent, then the consent must be in writing (Code D, para. 4.16), making answer D incorrect. The authorisation of an officer of the rank of inspector or above is not required, making answer C incorrect. Answer A is incorrect as a person may have their footwear impressions taken without consent if they are detained at a police station in consequence of being arrested for a recordable offence, charged with a recordable offence or informed they will be reported for a recordable offence and they have not had an impression of their footwear taken in the course of the investigation (unless the previous impression is not complete or of sufficient quality to allow satisfactory analysis, comparison or matching — whether in the case in question or generally) (Code D, para. 4.17).

Evidence and Procedure, para. 2.11.3.5

102. Answer **A** — Answers B, C and D are all incorrect. Answer B is incorrect because 'apprehension' does not mean 'fear' and there is no need to show that the actual victim was in fear. Answer C is wrong as the force required for a battery to be committed can be applied indirectly or directly (*Haystead* v *Chief Constable of Derbyshire* [2000] 3 All ER 890). Answer D is wrong because only a very small degree of physical contact is required for a battery to be committed.

Crime, para. 1.7.2.2

103. Answer **D** — Section 81(1) of the Road Traffic Regulation Act 1984 provides that the speed limit on a 'restricted road' will be 30 mph. A 'restricted road' in England and Wales (by virtue of s. 82 of the Act) is a road where there is provided on it a system of street lighting furnished by means of lamps placed not more than 200 yards apart.

Road Policing, para. 3.4.7.1

104. Answer **A** — A 'communication' can be in any form (including the Internet) making answer B incorrect. Answer C is incorrect as it is the intention of the person making the threat that is relevant to this offence and whether the person receiving it believes it or not is immaterial. This would seem to make answer D correct but this is not the case as the wording of the 1977 Act is in the present

tense and therefore a message threatening to place a bomb at a location sometime *in the future* would not suffice.

General Police Duties, para. 4.5.8.2

105. Answer **C** — In such circumstances, the shorter and alternative caution should be used, making answers A, B and D incorrect. The occasions where the alternative caution (as at answer C) is required are set out in Code C of the Codes of Practice. The alternative caution is required when there are restrictions on drawing an adverse inference, such as when a superintendent authorises an interview to go ahead without a solicitor being present and the person wants a solicitor.

Evidence and Procedure, paras 2.12.4 to 2.12.4.1

106. Answer **C** — Answer A is incorrect as a s. 18 PACE search can only be carried out at premises occupied or controlled by the person under arrest. Answer D is incorrect as the power under s. 19 of PACE is a power of seizure and not a power to search. A s. 32 PACE search may be conducted for the purpose of finding evidence relating to the offence for which the suspect was arrested. A police officer exercising a power under this section must have a genuine belief (i.e. more than mere suspicion) that there is evidence on the premises; it is not a licence for a general fishing expedition (*R* v *Beckford* [1991] Crim LR 918). This makes answer B incorrect.

General Police Duties, paras 4.4.13.1, 4.4.13.3, 4.4.15.1

107. Answer **D** — Trespassing with a weapon of offence can only be committed if the person concerned entered the premises as a trespasser. It does not therefore extend to a person who, having entered lawfully, then becomes a trespasser for whatever reason (e.g. because the occupier has told him/her to leave). As BOSS is not a trespasser when he enters the land or the house, the offence cannot be committed.

General Police Duties, para. 4.8.5

108. Answer **A** — The Regulation of Investigatory Powers (Directed Surveillance and Covert Human Intelligence Sources) Order 2003 (SI 2003/3171) as amended, sets out the relevant roles and ranks of the people in public authorities who can authorise directed surveillance. In the case of the police services, the relevant rank is superintendent, making answers C and D incorrect. Unless it is renewed, the authorisation given by a superintendent will ordinarily cease to have effect after three months beginning on the day that it was granted, making answer B incorrect.

General Police Duties, para. 4.12.4.5

109. Answer **B** — Vehicle interference is committed when a person interferes with a motor vehicle or trailer in order that a specific offence can be committed by him or some other person, making answer A incorrect. The defendant may have one of three ulterior offences in mind when the interference takes place: (i) theft of the motor vehicle or trailer, (ii) theft of anything carried in or on the motor vehicle or trailer, or (iii) an offence under s. 12(1) of the Theft Act 1968 (taking and driving away without consent), making answer C incorrect. The interference can be with a motor vehicle or a trailer as well as anything carried in or on it, making answer D incorrect.

Crime, para. 1.3.4.1

110. Answer **B** — This offence applies to firearms and imitation firearms. The offence is committed by a person having in his possession any firearm or imitation firearm with intent by means thereof to cause or to enable another person by means thereof to cause any person to believe that unlawful violence will be used against him or another person (s. 16A of the Firearms Act 1968). Therefore both THOMAS and HOWARD commit the offence.

General Police Duties, para. 4.7.8.2

111. Answer **D** — As answer D states, a person under 18 years should be tried and sentenced in the youth court, making answers A and B incorrect. Answer C is incorrect as a juvenile can be tried in a magistrates' court, e.g. when they are jointly charged with an adult.

VERIFICATION QUESTION, *Evidence and Procedure*, para. 2.2.3

112. Answer **A** — The offence under s. 3A of the Road Traffic Act 1988 is committed if a person causes the death of another by driving a mechanically propelled vehicle on a road or other public place without due care and attention, or without reasonable consideration for other persons using the road or place, and (under s. 3A(c)) he is, within 18 hours after that time, required to provide a specimen in pursuance of s. 7 of this Act, but without reasonable excuse fails to provide it. This makes answers C and D incorrect. The request must be made within 18 hours *after the driving which caused the death* and not after the death itself.

Road Policing, para. 3.2.7

113. Answer **D** — Answers A, B and C are incorrect as this would be classed as 'positive discrimination' (whereby people are selected in preference to others solely on the basis of their membership of a certain minority group). This is unlawful in England and Wales. An attempt to recruit female police officers into a specialist department by excluding male applicants was held to be unlawful in *Jones* v *Chief Constable of Northamptonshire Police* (1999), *The Times*, 1 November.

General Police Duties, paras 4.13.10.4, 4.13.11.2, 4.13.11.3

114. Answer **B** — This question is concerned with the definition of a 'building' for the purposes of burglary. A tent can never be a 'building' no matter what it is used for, making answer A incorrect. However, an unfinished house can be a 'building' making answer B the point where the offence is first committed and consequently making answers C and D incorrect.

Crime, para. 1.12.3.2

115. Answer **B** — The use of reg. 3 of the Removal and Disposal of Vehicles Regulations 1986 does not require the officer to be in uniform, making answer D incorrect. Answer A is incorrect as the power is applicable to the owner, the driver or other person in control or charge of the vehicle. Answer C is incorrect as the requirement to move the vehicle can be made not only where there is an actual obstruction but also where the vehicle is potentially obstructing other road users that may be expected at some time in the future (*Carey* v *Chief Constable of Avon & Somerset* [1995] RTR 405).

Road Policing, para. 3.8.6.2

116. Answer **C** — Service of a summons or requisition on a corporation may be undertaken by handing it to a person holding a senior position in the corporation or by leaving it at, or by sending it by first-class post to, its principal office in England and Wales.

Evidence and Procedure, para. 2.3.4

117. Answer **C** — Code C, para. 11.1, requires that an interview must take place at a police station or some other authorised place. However, the courts have recognised that this is not always the case and that there may be times when a person who is under arrest will be asked questions elsewhere than a police station, making answer A incorrect. In *R v Hanchard*, unreported, Case No. 99/1822/X4, December 6, 1999, CA, the courts recognised that searches of premises could not be carried out in complete silence. The court states that it would be unreasonable and unfair not to put any questions to owners of premises undergoing a search. However, what questions may be asked will be a matter of fact and degree in each case. Where questions go beyond that needed for the immediate investigation it would breach the Codes, making answer B incorrect. The questions asked of the suspect in *R v Hanchard* which were admissible included whether drugs at the address belonged to the suspect and where a large amount of money had come from, making answer D incorrect.

Evidence and Procedure, para. 2.12.6

118. Answer **D** — The Youth Justice Board was created by s. 41(1) of the Crime and Disorder Act 1998. The Board consists of up to 12 members appointed by the Secretary of State.

Evidence and Procedure, para. 2.6.5

119. Answer **D** — Answers A and C are incorrect as the offence of obtaining services dishonestly can only be committed if the service provided was made available on the basis that payment has been, or will be made for or in respect of them (s. 11(2)(a) of the Fraud Act 2006). In other words, services provided for free are not covered by the offence (answer D). Answer B is incorrect as this offence is a result crime and not a conduct crime — the offence does not require the defendant to practice a fraud or deception in order to obtain the service. Answer C is further incorrect as the sentence for this offence on summary conviction is a maximum of 12 months imprisonment.

Crime, para. 1.13.10

120. Answer **A** — It is a summary offence to park a vehicle in contravention of a prohibition or regulation imposed under s. 48 of the Terrorism Act 2000. It is a defence for a person charged with the offence under this section to prove that he/she had a reasonable excuse for the act or omission but possession of a current disabled person's badge is not itself a 'reasonable excuse' for these purposes, this makes answer C incorrect. It is also an offence if the driver or person in charge of any vehicle permits it to remain at rest in contravention of such a prohibition or restriction or fails to remove the vehicle when ordered to do so by a *constable in uniform*. Therefore, the request from DC TAPLOW carries no authority and answer D is incorrect. Answer B is incorrect (and also C and D for this reason) as an offence in contravention of the prohibitions or restrictions can only be committed if appropriate signs on the relevant road have been placed (s. 49).

Road Policing, para. 3.8.2.1

121. Answer **D** — Section 47 of the Road Traffic Act 1988 requires all motor vehicles which were first registered more than three years before the time they were being used on a road to pass a test. That requirement includes vehicles manufactured abroad (s. 47(2)(b)), making answer B incorrect. Some vehicles need to be tested after one year, notably:

- motor vehicles having more than eight seats (excluding the driver's seat) which are used to carry passengers (making answer A incorrect);
- taxis (answer D and the correct answer);
- ambulances (making answer C incorrect).

Road Policing, para. 3.9.6

122. Answer **A** — A person who, in respect of the offence, is or has been sentenced to a term of imprisonment for 30 months or more will be subject to notification requirements for an indefinite period (HUTTON). A person who, in respect of the offence, is or has been sentenced to a period of imprisonment for a term of more than six months but less than 30 months (FELIX) will be subject to notification requirements for 10 years.

Crime, para. 1.10.3.1

123. Answer **B** — The information of which NEWMAN is in possession would be classed as relating to 'terrorism' as defined in s. 1 of the Terrorism Act 2000. Answer A is incorrect as the disclosure of such information (in England and Wales) must be made to a constable. Answer C is incorrect as s. 38B(6) of the Act means that a person resident in the United Kingdom could be charged with the offence even if he/she was outside the country when he/she became aware of the information. Answer D is incorrect as it is a defence for a person charged with such an offence to prove that he/she has a reasonable excuse for not making the disclosure (s. 38B(4)).

General Police Duties, paras 4.6.14.2, 4.6.14.6

124. Answer **D** — This offence is committed when a person unlawfully intercepts a communication in the course of its transmission by means of a public postal service or a public telecommunication service, making answer A incorrect. The offence carries a maximum sentence of two years on indictment, making answer B incorrect. The interception can be accomplished by any means and does not need to be done electronically, making answer C incorrect.

General Police Duties, para. 4.12.4.6

125. Answer **B** — Answer A is incorrect as the offence is one of absolute liability and there is no need to prove intent or guilty knowledge. Answer C is incorrect as an insurance policy obtained by false representations will be valid for the purposes of s. 143 and will remain so until the contract has been 'avoided' (ended) by the insurer. Answer D is incorrect as there is a defence under s. 143 to this offence.

Road Policing, paras 3.6.2.1 to 3.6.2.3

126. Answer **B** — All three persons commit the offence in these circumstances. The motives of the individual do not matter, nor does the fact that SINGH printed the advert for free. Where a public advertisement offers a reward with no questions asked, the advertiser, printer and publisher of the advert all commit an offence.

Crime, para. 1.12.12

127. Answer **D** — Car parks are counted as 'other public places' which are included in the definition of a reportable accident under s. 170 of the Road Traffic Act 1988 (after the case of *Cutter* v *Eagle Star Insurance Co Ltd* [1998] 4 All ER 417). Whilst the damage to ZAHID's car is of no consequence as far as the Act is concerned, the injury to the passenger (shock is an injury under s. 170) is. As a person other than the driver has been injured owing to the presence of a motor vehicle in an 'other public place', this is a reportable accident. This makes answers A and C incorrect. Answer B is incorrect as the reporting of an accident must take place as soon as reasonably practicable and in any case within 24 hours of the accident. This does not give the driver up to 24 hours to report the accident.

Road Policing, paras 3.4.2 to 3.4.2.3

128. Answer **B** — Answers A and C are incorrect as this is not a s. 47 assault contrary to the Offences Against the Person Act 1861. Mild bruising (according to the CPS Charging Standards) would only constitute an offence under s. 39 of the Criminal Justice Act 1988. Answer D is incorrect as the Children Act 2004 (s. 58) whilst removing the defence of reasonable chastisement from more serious assault charges, still leaves the defence available for a defendant charged with a s. 39 assault on a child under the age of 16 years.

VERIFICATION QUESTION, *Crime*, paras 1.7.2.7 to 1.7.3.1

129. Answer **D** — The set of images on a video identification must include the suspect and at least eight other people who, so far as possible, resemble the suspect in age, general appearance and position in life. Only one suspect shall appear in any set unless there are two suspects of roughly similar appearance, in which case they may be shown together with at least 12 other people.

Evidence and Procedure, para. 2.11.2.8

130. Answer **C** — Section 30 of the Anti-social Behaviour Act 2003 allows an officer in uniform to remove any person under the age of 16 who is not under the effective control of a parent or a responsible person aged 18 or over to their place of residence. The power must only be used to protect children under 16 from the physical or social risks of anti-social behaviour by others or to prevent children from participating in anti-social behaviour themselves. However, the power is only available between the hours of 9 pm and 6 am and cannot be used in this situation.

General Police Duties, para. 4.6.12.3

131. Answer **C** — *R* v *G and R* [2003] 3 WLR 1060, effectively removed objective recklessness from criminal damage and replaced it with subjective recklessness. Under the old law, HYDE would have been considered reckless and although unlikely to be punished would be guilty of the offence. However, since *R* v *G and R* the approach would be different. As HYDE was unaware that a risk existed or would exist, he would not be reckless.

Crime, para. 1.1.4.2

132. Answer **A** — The offence is committed by RICE as a person commits this offence if, without lawful authority or reasonable excuse, the proof of which shall lie on him, he has in any public place any offensive weapon. A flick-knife is an offensive weapon *per se* and there is not a reasonable excuse to have such a weapon with you as a general precaution in case you are attacked; this makes answers B and D incorrect. BURTON does not commit the offence as per the decision in *Ohlson* v *Hylton* [1975]

1 WLR 724. Here the defendant had a bag of tools with him in the course of his trade and produced the hammer and hit someone with it. The court held that, as he had formed the intention to use the hammer after it came into his possession, the offence was not made out.

General Police Duties, paras 4.8.2 to 4.8.2.1

133. Answer **B** — Section 51(2) of the Sexual Offences Act 2003 redefined the term 'prostitute' and provides that a prostitute is a man or woman who on at least one occasion and whether or not compelled to do so, offers or provides a sexual service to another person in return for payment or a promise of payment to that or a third person. Therefore, answers A, C and D are all incorrect.

Crime, para. 1.9.11.1

134. Answer **D** — Although a specimen must be divided 'at the time' it is taken and as part of the same continuing event, there is no need for it to be done in the defendant's presence (*DPP* v *Elstob* [1992] Crim LR 518), making answer A incorrect. Answer B is incorrect as although the division of the specimen must be made at the time it is taken, there is no requirement for the defendant to be provided with his/her part 'at the time' — only that it be provided within a reasonable time thereafter (*R* v *Sharp* [1968] 2 QB 564). Answer C is incorrect as the Administrative Court has held that there is no freestanding right, either under the Road Traffic Offenders Act 1988 or at common law, for the defendant to be informed of his/her entitlement to a part of the sample. In *R* v *Ash* [1999] RTR 347, the Court of Appeal refused to extend the requirements of s. 15(5) to an offence of causing death by dangerous driving.

Road Policing, para. 3.5.8.4

135. Answer **D** — A CHIS is someone who establishes or maintains a relationship with another person for the covert purpose of obtaining information or providing access to information, or covertly discloses information obtained by the use of such a relationship. A 'covert' relationship is one where the relationship (and the subsequent disclosure of information) is conducted in a manner that is calculated to ensure that one of the parties is unaware of that purpose (s. 26(9) of the Regulation of Investigatory Powers Act 2000). This definition means that answer B is incorrect as MARSHALL's activities would be classed as 'covert'. People who have come across information in the ordinary course of their jobs and suspect criminal activity (such as bank staff) do not have a covert relationship with the police simply by passing on information. However, answers A and C are incorrect as if the person supplying information is asked by the police to do something further to develop or enhance it (i.e. tasked by the police), this could make the person a CHIS.

General Police Duties, para. 4.12.4.4

136. Answer **A** — Section 7(5) of the Human Rights Act 1998 states that proceedings must be brought before the end of: (a) the period one year beginning with the date on which the act complained of took place; or (b) such longer period as the court or tribunal considers equitable having regard to all the circumstances.

General Police Duties, para. 4.3.3.6

137. Answer **C** — Answer B is incorrect as the requirement under s. 27 of the Police and Criminal Evidence Act 1984 can be made if the fingerprints obtained on the previous occasion are of insufficient quality to allow satisfactory analysis, comparison or matching. The requirement can be made of a person

convicted of a recordable offence, or given a caution in respect of a recordable offence which, at the time of the caution, the person admitted, or warned or reprimanded under s. 65 of the Crime and Disorder Act 1998, for a recordable offence, making answer D incorrect. Answer A is incorrect as the period in which HADDON would have to attend is seven days.

Evidence and Procedure, para. 2.11.3.2

138. Answer **D** — What amounts to a 'reasonable excuse' is a matter of law; whether the defendant actually had such an excuse is a question of fact for the court to determine, having regard to the particular circumstances of the case. There have been many cases where 'excuses' have been put forward. Answers A, B and C have all been held *not* to be a reasonable excuse for failing to provide a specimen under this section. Answer D has been held to be a reasonable excuse.

Road Policing, para. 3.5.6.1

139. Answer **D** — A person who, without lawful authority, uses or threatens violence to secure entry for himself or another is guilty of an offence provided that there is somebody on the premises at the time who is opposed to the entry which the violence is intended to secure and the person using or threatening the violence knows that is the case. This means that if there is nobody on the premises the offence is not committed and so WITHERS cannot be guilty, making answers B and C incorrect. This section would not apply to a 'displaced residential occupier' (HAMILTON), making answer A incorrect or a person acting on their behalf (WITHERS) making answers B and C further incorrect.

VERIFICATION QUESTION, *General Police Duties*, paras 4.10.9.3, 4.10.9.4

140. Answer **B** — The maximum magistrates' court custody time limit (from first appearance to start of trial) is 56 days.

Evidence and Procedure, para. 2.5.7.3

141. Answer **B** — Surveillance is intrusive if it is covert, carried out in relation to anything taking place on any residential premises or in any private vehicle and involves the presence of an individual on the premises or in the vehicle, or is carried out by way of a surveillance device. The extent of the definition of 'residential premises' is much wider than that of the conventional home. The use of specialist devices in hotel rooms will generally fall into the category of intrusive surveillance. The fact that the device is not actually *on or in* the premises will not change the type of surveillance if the device used consistently provides information of the same quality and detail as might be expected from a device that was actually present on the premises or in the vehicle (s. 26(5) of the Regulation of Investigatory Powers Act 2000). Therefore, answers A and D are incorrect. Answer C is incorrect as it is clear from the wording of s. 26 of the Act that surveillance must be one or the other; it cannot be both.

General Police Duties, para. 4.12.4.5

142. Answer **A** — All the suspect needs to do is to provide an account to the interviewing officer. It does not matter whether the interviewing officer believes it, making answer B incorrect. Answer C is incorrect as 'special warnings' are not limited to offences involving dishonesty. A solicitor does not need to be present for a 'special warning' to be given, making answer D incorrect.

Evidence and Procedure, para. 2.7.6.3

143. Answer **C** — The defence of duress is not available in respect of an offence of murder (*R v Howe* [1987] AC 417). Answer A is incorrect as the threat can be made to 'loved ones'. Answer B is incorrect as although the threat drove CAVELL to commit the offence this is just one of the requirements and answer A supersedes this. Answer D is not correct as the requirement relating to time (imminently) relates to the threatened injury to the defendant or his/her 'loved ones'.

Crime, para. 1.4.6

144. Answer **C** — Child safety orders relate to children under the age of 10 years, making answer A incorrect. There is a right of appeal to the High Court against a magistrates' court making a child safety order, making answer B incorrect. Answer D is incorrect as there is no minimum age for an order.

Evidence and Procedure, paras 2.6.8 to 2.6.8.1

145. Answer **C** — Section 24 of the Youth Justice and Criminal Evidence Act 1999 provides for the use of a live television link as part of a series of special measures to assist young, disabled or intimidated witnesses give evidence in criminal proceedings. Special measures are not limited to those suffering from mental or physical disorders, making answer D incorrect. This section relates to witnesses in the Crown Court but only to vulnerable witnesses (s. 16) in the magistrates' court, this makes answer B incorrect. A vulnerable witness under s. 16 of the Act is a witness who is under the age of 17 at the time of the hearing (RUPPERT) or a witness who suffers from a mental or physical disorder. An intimidated witness is a witness whose evidence is likely to be affected on the grounds of fear or distress about testifying (BARN). BARN is not a vulnerable witness and would not be allowed to give evidence via a live television link, making answer A incorrect.

Evidence and Procedure, paras 2.5.10.1, 2.5.10.3.

146. Answer **A** — The offence of aggravated vehicle taking is committed when the 'basic offence' of taking a conveyance is committed and at any time after that taking and before it was recovered, the vehicle was:

(a) driven dangerously on a road or public place;
(b) that owing to the driving of the vehicle, an accident occurred by which injury was caused to any person;
(c) that, owing to the driving of the vehicle, an accident occurred by which damage was caused to any property, other than the vehicle;
(d) that damage was caused to the vehicle.

If *any one* of these consequences occurs then the person commits the offence. Therefore, answers B, C and D are wrong. In respect of the accident, it does not matter that STIRK was driving in a sedate and responsible fashion — s. 12A is concerned with consequences and not with how those consequences came about. Should CHEN die from the injuries received, STIRK's sentence could increase to 14 years' imprisonment.

Crime, paras 1.12.6 to 1.12.6.1

147. Answer **C** — The offence might be termed 'driving or riding on a *motor cycle* in contravention of Regulations' but the Regulations do not apply to all motor cycles; they only apply to motor bicycles. A motor bicycle is a two-wheeled motor cycle, whether having a side-car attached to it or not. Therefore the Regulations apply to the motor bicycle that MATRON is driving. The helmet should not

be worn unfastened or improperly fastened so MATRON commits an offence, making answers B and D incorrect. TOLLY has not committed an offence as s. 16(1) of the Road Traffic Act exempts people in sidecars from the Regulations, making answer A incorrect.

Road Policing, para. 3.7.3

148. Answer **C** — Violent disorder is committed when three or more persons, who are present together, use or threaten unlawful violence and the conduct of them (taken together) is such as would cause a person of reasonable firmness present at the scene to fear for his personal safety (s. 3(1) of the Public Order Act 1986). It is immaterial whether the three use or threaten violence simultaneously (s. 3(2)).

General Police Duties, para. 4.6.5

149. Answer **B** — Answer A is incorrect as a strip-search does not require the authority of an inspector or above. Answer C is incorrect as a search should only take place if the custody officer reasonably believes that the detained person might have concealed an article which he/she would not be allowed to keep. Answer D is incorrect as the removal of socks and shoes would not be considered a strip-search.

Evidence and Procedure, para. 2.10.11.11

150. Answer **B** — Section 5.7 to 5.10 of the Code of Practice under Part II of the Criminal Procedure and Investigations Act 1996 states that where the accused is convicted, all material which may be relevant must be retained at least until the convicted person is released from custody (where the court imposes a custodial sentence).

Evidence and Procedure, para. 2.9.6.11